For The Wife Woman, for enduring my strangeness for the past 37 years

It's A Strange Place, England

It's A Strange Place, England

Jack's Strange Tales Book 2

Jack Strange

Contents

Introduction
Even the Language is Strange

It's a strange place, England. It occupies much of the southern two-thirds of the island of Great Britain, with a world-class capital in London, a host of vibrant cities and a history that stretches as far back as Stonehenge and probably further. Yet people see the epitome of Englishness as a fondness for quaint little villages of thatched cottages, cricket games on the village green, tea at the Vicarage and a quiet pint of beer at the local public house. All of which is good, except that the little villages will undoubtedly have a history of smugglers or highwaymen and the pub will invariably have a ghost or two. England is like that.

England is a thrusting country that wraps itself in its past, a place where grim castles built by Norman conquerors now sit at peace in some of the loveliest countryside anywhere. It is a country where the ghosts of Empire glide across a land crossed by six-lane motorways and the maritime past is remembered in coastal towns boasting expensive housing. It is a country of constant oxymorons, a green land of industry, and a quaint land of monsters and welcoming museums where smiling curators will guide visitors through a history as savage as any in the world.

Possibly the strangest thing about England is the fact that some English people do not know its borders. There are some who confuse England with Great Britain and use the terms indiscriminately. As a major part of the political union of Great Britain, England has much to be proud of without trying to lay claim to the other British nations as well. It is also strange that some call it an island nation when England is not an island. It has land borders with Wales and Scotland. How strange is that? So for clarification: England is a country of some 55 million people and part of a political union that comprises Scotland, Wales England and Northern Ireland. These are four countries that share a queen and a parliament. This book is only about England and not the others.

There: that's that said, so it's time to get on with the writing.

The nation of England is scarcely over eleven hundred years old. Before that, it was a patchwork of little kingdoms, most of which have been blotted from memory so even academics would have trouble working out where the boundaries were. When the Romans invaded the British Isles in 43 AD, England did not exist. The English were still pagan tribesmen in far-off Germania, having not yet surged westward to invade Britain. The old British tribes had names such as Brigantes, Iceni and Cornovii (from which latter tribe we can recognise Cornwall). After the withdrawal of Rome, and the invasion of the Germanic tribes of Angles, Jutes and Saxons from continental Europe in the sixth century, individual war-lords carved out small mini-kingdoms. Many of these are now counties or recognisable areas: Sussex, the land of the South Saxons, Essex, the land of the East Saxons, East Anglia where the East Angles were, Northumberland, the land north of the Humber. Others, such as Deira, Lindsey and Bernicia have faded from memory.

Mergers and conquest led to the formation of larger Angle or Saxon kingdoms, such as Wessex, home of the West Saxons, Mercia, ruled by the pagan Penda, while the indigenous British strived to hold onto their lands in the face of the merciless invaders. There was Cumbria, where the Cymric-speaking Britons lived, and Rheged around the shores of the Solway. There was also the less obvious divides, one of which was the River Parrett in Somerset. This river was the agreed boundary between the pixies and the fairies. On the west were the pixies, these red-haired, broad-faced creatures with green clothes who stole horses and enticed travellers off their paths, while to the west were the fairies, mythical creatures whom it was best to avoid. In early England, it was sometimes difficult to know where legend and myth end and where history begins.

Take King Arthur for instance. To some, he is an English folk-hero, to others the chivalric knight in Malory's *Le Morte D'Arthur* while those historians who believe he existed – and the jury is still out on that – think he was an indigenous British warlord battling against the tide of English invasion. Even where he operated is unclear; it may have been the English West Country, middle England, North West England or out of England completely in Wales or southern Scotland. It is strange to think that historians cannot accurately place such an iconic character as King Arthur. It is also intriguing, just one mystery in a land of strangeness.

Another strange thing is the food of the nation. Continentals have scorned English food in the recent past, yet only a couple of hundred years ago each region of the country had local fare that was both unique and worth sampling. The jellied eels of Thames-side London should be well known, while Lancashire hot-pot, Cornish pasties and Yorkshire puddings are still famous. But birds were also once eaten, with woodcock, snipe, plover and great bustards on the bills-of-fare of many eighteenth and nineteenth century inns, and boars, hare and venison were fairly standard. Add little-known fish delicacies such as elvers and lampreys, pike, chub and carp, and today's menus seem dull in comparison. Even worse; Cambridge brawn, Somerset laver, Banbury cheese and Kentish huffkins are hardly known now; what delicacies have been lost in the progress of time.

These are only some aspects of a country riddled with the strange and the curious, from haunted places and traditions that go back centuries, with memories of some extraordinary people and events and with sports and games that stretch credulity. For example, there was one of the most famous mass murderers in history in Jack the Ripper, there are the world black-pudding throwing championships, and there is a screaming skull that refuses to leave its home. There was the Mad Major who rehearsed his own funeral and Springheeled Jack who bounced around the countryside terrorising people.

Despite all the strangeness, England has given some wonderful things to the world. As well as parliamentary democracy, cricket and rugby, one of the great gifts that England had bestowed on humanity is the English language. It is an international language used by businesses the world over and is capable of tremendous flexibility. From the northernmost tip of Canada to South Island New Zealand and from Shetland to the Falkland Islands, England is spoken and understood by millions. But just how English is the English language?

The base is English of course or rather Anglo-Saxon from the Germanic tribes that invaded Britain in the sixth and seventh centuries AD and made the southern and eastern part of the British Isles their own. However many of the words that are in daily use have been added through time and reveal the journey that the English people have made from Germanic invader of the Celtic lands to a permanent nation- state, trading nation, part of the United Kingdom, headquarters of Imperial Britain and then back to a portion of Britain. The language is a picture of progress that offers a fascinating insight into the history of a people.

We will look at some English words first. Take the word *know* for instance. Have you ever wondered why there is a silent 'k' at the beginning? That is because the original word was *kenow*. In the northern part of the Anglo-Saxon world the second half, the *ow* sound was dropped, and the word became *ken* while in the southern part the *e* was dropped and the word became *know*. Not many people *kenow* those facts.

Or how about the quaint old *ye* for *the*? From where does that come? Well – it comes from English itself. In Early Modern English, scribes frequently recorded the word *the* as þe with þ being a no-longer-used Old English letter called *thorn*, a simple single character for the 'th' sound. When people put the letters into print þ and y look very similar and were often mixed up. So that explains that.

Other so-called English words have entered the language from other languages and countries. *Smashing* and *clan* come from Gaelic either through the English colonial attempts in Ireland or the influence of Highland Scots. Other words also have Gaelic origins such as *slogan*, the war cry of a particular clan. Lowland Scotland also gave *blackmail* – which meant payment by cattle rather than by cash – and *feud*, a minor war between families or clans. *Galore* is another Gaelic word often used in English and less obviously, so is *trousers*, which has replaced the old-fashioned word *breeches* in English.

Others come from further afield in the days of empire.

For example, when the English settlers and traders mingled with the Inuit of eastern Canada they adopted local words which later eased into the English language without demur. That is how terms such as *kayak* and *parka* eased into everyday use. Centuries of association with the Native Americans brought *moccasin* and *canoe*, as well as names for well-known vegetables and fruit such as *potato* and *tomato*, with *maize* added to taste. Potatoes are so much part of English culture it is hard to imagine life without bangers and mash, or fish and chips, yet both would be impossible without the overseas connection. Another traditional English habit, although less common nowadays, is drinking *cocoa*, which is also a Native American word as is the more sinister *cocaine*. Although some people may think that *barbecue* is an Australian word, it is from Central America, as is *can-*

nibal, from the Carib people who gave their name to the Caribbean. Less obvious is the word *shack*, now meaning a slightly run-down hut. The English language becomes less English by the word!

Of all the places from trade and empire, perhaps it is India that has provided most words that we now accept as English. The words from that sub-continent are varied and many. For example, an *avatar* is in frequent use yet its first meaning was from Hindi and was a deity from heaven. In daily use is the word *bungalow*, which is the Hindi word for a house 'in the Bengal style' with a single storey. Other words we frequently use, and without thought, but which came from India include *pyjamas, shampoo* and *chutney* (which was the Urdu word to crush), with the obvious addition of *curry*. All are now as much part of the English language as the French words *bouquet, brunette, café, debacle, entrepreneur* and *reservoir*.

Perhaps less obviously Indian is the word *dinghy*, a small boat, which passed into English together with the word *jungle*, meaning wilderness. And very few people would realise that *loot* is another Urdu word, again having retained nearly its original meaning of 'to steal'. The Hindu word *yoga* has entirely retained its original meaning, while *cot* has altered only slightly from its correct designation of a hammock. Another Indian importee is the word *thug* from the religion of *thag* or *thugee* that saw one particular religious sect strangling and dismembering travellers in the name of their god. Today the word has become debased and means a mindless, brutal and violent person.

While it would not be hard to guess that *bazaar* is an Indian word, few would know that *pundit* is from Urdu; all these sports *pundits* are labelled with a foreign language while many of them struggle with basic English! *Toddy* sounds more Scottish than Indian – nothing like a hot *toddy* with whisky, hot water and honey to fight a sore throat and the onset of a cold.

Trade with China and perhaps missionary work or the occupation of Hong Kong saw the introduction of a number of Chinese words into English. Some are obvious such as *silk* and *tea*, the latter which also become a staple of English society, while *ketchup* is a substance spattered on fish and chips without the user being aware of the oriental origins of the word. *Tycoon* and *typhoon* also come from China.

Africa has also given its quota of words such as *banana* and the less obvious *cola*, while few people will not be aware of *zombies* in film and literature. The word *trek* came from the Boer settlers in South Africa, another area of colonisation. This word has not altered its meaning much.

With all these words and many more prevalent in the language we speak, it is strange that it is known as *English* and not as *International*. On the other hand, such a fusion of words proves the viability and dynamism of the language and shows yet again why English is spoken so widely throughout the world.

To take things one step further, from where do our common expressions come? The things we say each day without thinking? Well, they originated in different places, from occupations and work, warfare and daily events. There are too many to repeat them all, but a few examples will give a flavour of the depth of history that common everyday expressions hide.

For example *rummaging* and *the coast is clear* are from the days of smuggling, with the customs officers *rummaging* through ships to search for contraband and smugglers looking out for revenue cutters before landing their illicit goods. Of course, the old sailing navy brought a whole host of terms from *to swing a cat* to *three sheets in the wind.* The cat in question was of the cat-o-nine-tails variety and not the four-legged purring type, while people three sheets in the wind are drunk and unsteady, as any vessel would be if she had three sheets in that condition. Many people will know the old expression *cold enough to freeze the balls off a brass monkey* yet few will know from where it originates. The initial image that may spring to mind is a very uncomfortable looking monkey with his hands tightly folded in front of itself and an expression of intense anguish on his little face. However, the reality is somewhat different.

In the old days of a sail-powered navy, Royal Navy ships protected the whaling vessels in the Arctic Ocean and also conveyed merchant vessels to and from the Baltic. The Royal Navy ships carried cannon, which fired iron balls. The Navy stored these cannonballs in a contraption known as a monkey. In the case of a flagship – the vessel of a commodore or above – the monkeys could be made of brass. Now brass does not shrink with the cold but iron does, so when the weather was bitterly cold the iron cannon balls could contract and slip between the brass bars of the monkey, so making it cold enough to freeze the balls off a brass monkey. Nothing crude at all!

One expression which people seldom use now is *son of a gun* yet at one time it was fairly common. It also comes from the days of the old sailing navy. Warships in Nelson's time, and for decades before and after, did not only carry men. Most would have a quota of women on board as well, the wives of petty officers and specialists such as carpenters, sailmakers and the like. Inevitably with women and men together, some women would fall pregnant on the voyage and would have to give birth on board. This perilous operation would take place behind a canvas screen, next to the midships cannon and if the father was unknown, the child would become a *son of a gun.*

The term *blazer* meaning a bright jacket comes from HMS *Blazer*, whose commander issued his men with striped jackets to wear, while *clear the decks* was to get rid of any extraneous material so the ship could fight more efficiently. How about *turning a blind eye*? Blame Admiral Nelson for that one when he put his telescope to his blind eye at the battle of Copenhagen and pretended he did not see a signal ordering him not to engage. He did engage and won the battle. There are many more such phrases from the days of sail.

All sorts of activities have added to the fund of expressions used in the English language. The phrase *gone west* meaning to die is said to come from the direction in which convicted criminals were transported to the gallows at Tyburn for the hangman to string them up. *Bite the bullet* comes from wounded men in war before the use of anaesthetic when the only way to fight the agony of amputation or other surgical operations was to bite on a leather belt or a lead musket ball. *Mad as a hatter* means just that: hatters used mercury in their trade and the resulting poisoning made them foul-tempered and shy. *Barking up the wrong tree* was a hunting expression when a pack of dogs treed the quarry but gathered around the trunk of a different tree.

Bury the hatchet comes from the negotiations between British colonists and Native Americans who would literally bury their hatchets – their weapons – to show their peaceful intentions. *Caught red-handed* – well that comes from the middle ages when the landed gentry forbade anybody except themselves from hunting on their land. An ordinary man caught with the blood from a poached animal still in his hands could expect an extreme penalty. Another medieval saying is to *let your hair down*, when the ladies of the castles could finally relax and undo their elaborate hair-dos.

How about the expression *beyond the pale*? That comes from the English occupation of Ireland. The English conquered the area around Dublin and erected a fence, a paling, to mark where their territory ended, and that of the Wild Irish – or free Irish - began. Beyond this pale was land controlled by the Irish clans and therefore dangerous to the English invaders. Finally, there is the old statement a *flash in the pan*, meaning a one-off that did not lead to anything. That comes from the old flintlock muskets when the flint ignited a trail of gunpowder that led to the charge that propelled the lead ball. If the powder in the pan merely flashed without igniting the trail to the ball, the musket did not fire.

Some expressions have been lost, which may not be a bad thing. Is there a modern criminal who could match the highwayman's cheerful: 'you suffocated dogs-in-doublets and sodomitical sons of bitches – hand over your cash?'

All these words and expressions show something from the history of the strange country of England. They reveal the history and traditions but only hint at the genuine strangeness that permeates every town, every county and nearly every day of life in Strange England. Read on...

Chapter One
Strange Ghosty Things

Ghost stories are always popular, and England has more than its share. After all, one of the world's most famous ghost stories, Dicken's *A Christmas Carol: A Ghost Story of Christmas* was published as early as 1843, while that other English writer, William Shakespeare, introduces a ghost in *Hamlet*. From the stern islands off Northumberland to the wind-battered coasts of Cornwall, from the fells of Cumbria to the gentle downland and hushing seas of the south, England can boast of its ghosts. As it would take an encyclopaedia to catalogue them all, this chapter will relate only a representative sample.

Situated nearly at the furthermost point of Northern England, Lindisfarne, or Holy Island is a place that would be unique in whichever country it blessed. This tidal island with its priory and mediaeval castle is a mecca for tourists who come for the unique atmosphere, the cosy little hotels and the famous Lindisfarne Mead. Some also visit to experience the history and a few may even hope to meet the ghosts, of which there are many.

The priory in Lindisfarne is in ruins now but once it shone as a beacon of Christian hope in a very dark world of paganism and brutality. In 635 AD Aidan from the Scottish island of Iona founded this holy place. His mission was to spread Christianity to the Woden-worshipers of Anglian Northumberland – the land north of the Humber River. On Aidan's death, St Cuthbert from Melrose in the Scottish Borders took over. There are many tales about Cuthbert, including the time he sought solitude in the Farne Islands only to find them infested with noisy goblins. The saint sent them to the offshore islets, but the noises continued and the goblins resorted to riding on goats. However, Cuthbert persisted with his prayers, befriending seals and the odd sea monster while his fellow monks from Lindisfarne spread the word of God. Apparently, Cuthbert was the first to find the causeway to Lindisfarne while the socket of his cross, the Petting Stone, was so blessed that newlywed couples jumped over it to ensure a happy marriage.

Being peaceful and relatively wealthy Holy Island naturally became a target for raiding Norsemen. The *Anglo-Saxon Chronicle* for 793 reads like this:

This year came dreadful fore-warnings over the land of the Northumbrians, terrifying the people most woefully: these were immense sheets of light rushing through the air, and whirlwinds, and fiery dragons flying across the firmament. These tremendous tokens were soon followed by a great famine: and not long after, on the sixth day before the ides of January in the same year, the harrowing inroads of heathen men made lamentable havoc in the church of God in Holy-island, by rapine and slaughter.

The Norse came by the ship-load with sword and steel, fire and murder. The monks had no chance against professional sea-raiders, and they withdrew, leaving the island to the seagulls and questing seals. For decade after decade, the wind held dominion over the holy island as the dragon-ships slid by on their quest for gold and glory. The essence of the saints remained, gliding over the sea-polished shingle as they watched the light they had started flicker and fade, and then gleam again in a candle-glitter among the blood-dark of the Middle Ages.

In 1082 with the long swords and plunging lances of William of Normandy's knights, conquering Saxon England, Christianity returned to Lindisfarne in the shape of Benedictine monks. A priory was built stone by precious stone, and the light of hope shone once more across the tossing seas of the north. Generations of the devout and the pious walked here and the music of prayer mingled with the call of seabirds and the sonorous hush of the waves. Some, however, were reluctant to leave and remained even after death, with their spirits merging with the grey stones.

As well as the priory, the island has a castle, presumably created in an attempt to guard the island from pirates or predatory Scots, for Lindisfarne is only a few miles south of the much-disputed Border between England and Scotland. Unlike the priory, the castle is intact, with the owners restoring it as recently as 1902. It sits on a prominent rock above the shore, a dominant presence in the outline of the island and a target for visitors.

So much for geography and history; how abo strange part? It would be unusual if there were r in such a place. Arguably the best known is t

St Cuthbert, who drifts around the shattered remnants of the priory and wanders along the shore close to the castle. There is said to be one particular stone slab on which he stands in the priory, but disagreement about exactly which stone this is. The best time to see the restless saint is when a high tide washes the long beaches and a full moon acts as nature's lantern in these vast, cool skies. Even if one does not see the ghost, such a night brings tremendous beauty to the island so the expedition will never be a waste of time.

The moon may shine on St Cuthbert or on the ghostly hound that also prowls the ruins and occasionally lunges at tourists. Although there have no reports of anybody being killed or even severely bitten it may be an idea to carry a few biscuits in case this canine ghost is hungry. There is said to be another monk on or near the tidal causeway that leads to the mainland. Either he lost the road and was caught by the rising tide, or he is watching for somebody coming to the island. Either way, he is harmless.

There are even more monks at the priory, including one who walks through a wall, which is always a trick worth seeing, but most stories come back to St Cuthbert. He can be heard on dark nights while the wind whistles through the battered remains of the priory and the sea crashes against the rocky shore. Listen for him hammering on the stones, making Cuddy's beads –or St Cuthbert's Beads to give them an official name. The wearer of these beads will carry the saint's blessing.

St Cuthbert's ghost has been around a long time. When King Alfred – he of the burnt cakes- was a fugitive in Northumberland, a long way from his Wessex home, he bumped into Cuthbert, who assured him that he would eventually gain victory and gain the kingship of England. Every schoolboy knows that Alfred became great and did plant his regal posterior on the throne, but only of Wessex, not of all England for the Danes ruled the northern half. Still, even saints can't be right all the time.

The castle at Lindisfarne also has a ghost, of course. There is a spectral soldier still at the post he has occupied since the 1640s when he was part of the Royalist garrison holding the castle against Cromwell's Roundheads. Other versions say that the ghost was one of Cromwell's men. Perhaps somebody can clear up the mystery by asking the lonely sentinel, whose tour of duty should surely end soon.

The island is also the home of a ghostly nun with the lovely name of Constance de Beverley. According to legend, she fell in love with a soldier, which was not allowed, and she was either executed for her crime or was so distraught at being torn between her faith and her humanity that she can never find rest. Either way, visitors can sometimes meet her roaming through the nights.

Naturally, there is more to Lindisfarne than just a few ghosts. This holiest of all English islands was also a fishing station and used to profit from tragedy. When storms forced ships onto the rocks, the locals liked nothing more than to plunder the wrecks. One local man told me that when an eighteenth-century minister used to pray, he asked the Lord that if he must create shipwrecks, could he please send them in his direction. A strange request for a man of God.

This northern section of England can lay claim to a plethora of fascinating spirits, which is not at all prising given its history. One of the most distinctive of Northumberland's, indeed England's ancient monuments is Hadrian's Wall, built from AD 122 by the Romans to keep out the untamed tribes from the North, or perhaps to keep the unhappy natives from the South within Rome's peace. Either way, this marvel of ancient military engineering is haunted.

High above the seventy-three mile long Wall, the unlucky may see a host of *something* searching for human souls. These things, animals, spirits or a mixture of both, are known as the Wild Hunt and are seen or heard or felt the length and breadth of England. The Hunt above Hadrian's Wall seems to have no description but is obviously best avoided. This Wild Hunt also passes by Haltwhistle on occasion and apparently makes dogs and cats most upset.

More tangible, or more often seen, is the Roman soldier who remains on guard at Milecastle 42, perhaps better known as Cawfields Milecastle. The Romans built these milecastles at regular intervals along the wall as patrol bases or resting posts for sentries. Imagine coming from North Africa or Southern Italy and ending up patrolling this wall in a Northumberland winter: the sentries would be in utter misery as they huddled from the biting northern wind and stared into the misty hill-country where the un-tamed Picts lived. To men from the sun-kissed south, the Wall must have seemed like the last outpost on Earth.

The soldier in Milecastle 42 has not yet returned home although he has long been a time-expired man. He is seen in daylight, hovering around sixteen feet above ground, which was the level of the wall when the legions were on patrol. There is a story attached that claims his name is

Lucius and he fell in love with a local British girl. However, although she seemed to return his affection, she was fickle and used their relationship to enable her brother to smuggle goods over the border to the free lands of the north. Eventually, the Romans captured the brother, and the story came out. Realising that his lover was false, Lucius committed suicide and was doomed to guard forever the borders of an Empire that has long since ceased to exist.

Romans haunt other parts of England too, with an entire legion seen marching near Bleaklow Hill in Derbyshire. Perhaps they are relieving the garrison of the old Roman Forts at Glossop and Brough, or some unkind general sent them on a route-march for some minor misdemeanour. Every bit as entertaining is the Roman soldier who marches at Wroxham in Norfolk. People have seen him in spring, summer and autumn although never in winter. He is an authoritarian ghost who may command the watcher to disappear, which would be a pity, for this particular Roman is only the precursor of a whole circus that includes gladiators, chariots, lions and slaves, all on their eternal journey to the arena the Romans built in this area. Kenchester in Herefordshire is another place where Roman soldiers are still on the march, and sometimes even stop to camp. The Roman Empire may have long withdrawn from the green fields of England, but many of its guardians seem reluctant to return home.

To return to the north, not far from Hadrian's Wall at Haltwhistle is Bellister Castle. A 'grey man' haunts this castle, and legend claims that he was a harper. According to the story, the man was a wandering minstrel who sat in a corner and played his harp.

Walter Scott's Lay of the Last Minster comes to mind:

The way was long, the wind was cold,
The Minstrel was infirm and old

However, in this occasion, the place was so unfriendly that the harper decided to leave early, which made the Lord of Bellister think he was a spy. Sending his dogs after the minstrel, His Lordship watched as they tore the innocent man to pieces. His screams are still sometimes heard, together with the growling and baying of the dogs. If the ghost is not grisly enough, then visitors to the castle can peruse the old sycamore in the garden, where supporters of King Charles I hanged their Roundhead enemies during the Civil War of the seventeenth century.

Not surprisingly given the history of the area, northern England holds many haunted castles. One ghost with a slightly more concrete story is that is Archie Armstrong. In the sixteenth century, the old Border between England and Scotland was a turbulent place, with the so-called Riding Families of both nations indulging in reiving and feuding. Both these activities could involve men from either side of the Border, and the raids could be directed into Scotland or against England. Of all the Border reiving surnames, the Armstrongs were amongst the most notorious, able to raise as many as three thousand men when pushed. Their main base was Liddesdale on the Scottish side of the Border although they were an international family with branches in England as well.

One of these wild men from Liddesdale, Archie Armstrong had a reputation for extreme lawlessness. Tynedale was a favourite hunting ground, and on one fatal occasion Sir Thomas Swinburne of Haughton Castle captured Archie and threw him into a dungeon. Swinburne made sure he was well locked up and then left to meet Cardinal Wolsey in York. Unfortunately, he carried the dungeon key with him, and when he returned, Archie Armstrong had starved to death.

By the time Swinburne opened the door, Armstrong was already dead and had gnawed at his arm in his desperate hunger. Ever since then, Armstrong's ghost has haunted Haughton, with terrible screams coming from the dungeon where he died. However, that is not the end of the story.

When the ghost's yelling got too disturbing, the lord of the castle sent for a priest, who performed an exorcism. Archie's ghost departed, and the priest left a black leather- covered Bible as surety that it did not return. For many years the castle remained peaceful, and then the Bible, old and battered was removed to be re-bound. That was not a good idea as the screaming and yelling began again. It was so obvious that Archie Armstrong was not at peace that the lord of the castle returned the Bible, and since then the dungeon has been quiet.

Armstrong is not the only screaming ghost in England. There is another much further south in Bettiscombe Manor near Lyme Regis in Dorset. The story here is complicated and, as often happens, there is more than one version.

The original story seems to jog along like this:

King James II was an unpopular monarch because of his Catholicism at a time that the vast majority of people were Protestant. In 1685 the Duke of Monmouth led a revolt against the king in the West Country, with the lord of Bettiscombe Manor, a man with the charming name of Azariah Pinney, in full support. The revolt failed, and an unkind judge banished Pinney, who we will meet again in a later chapter, to the sugar islands of the Caribbean. That may not sound like much of a punishment, but at that time the West Indies were extremely unhealthy with tropical diseases for which there was as yet no cure. Pinney flourished and came home a wealthy man, bringing with him one of his slaves.

The slave was most likely an African but could have been a native of the Caribbean islands – accounts differ. It appears that the climate of England did not agree with him and he sickened. When he was close to death, he requested that Pinney should return his body to his native home. Would that be the Caribbean or Africa, one wonders? Some versions of the story say that he said if Pinney failed to return the slave's body, there would be a curse on Bettiscombe. Shortly before the slave died, Pinney agreed that he would fulfil his request.

Despite his promise, Pinney had the slave buried in the local churchyard, a long way from his home. That proved to be a big mistake, for the dead slave immediately began to scream and moan from his grave. Naturally, the local population were upset and asked Pinney to do something about it – quickly. He responded by having the body dug up and placed in a loft in the manor house. In time it decomposed until only the skull remained, or perhaps the rest of the body was indeed shipped home to be buried.

The skull began to scream. Every time somebody carried it out of the house, it emitted a terrible noise and was hurried back inside again. Different people tried various methods of getting rid of the skull. One man threw it into a pond and hoped that would cure the noises. He was wrong; all night yells and screams resounded around him so he could not sleep. The next day he dredged the pond for the skull and replaced it inside the house. The screams ended at once.

Even with the skull in place, strange things happen. One night each year a phantom coach is seen racing from the manor to the churchyard, known as the 'funeral procession of the skull'.

When brave volunteers have tried to sleep in the same room as the skull, they all report terrible nightmares and apparently nobody has gone back a second time. Only the owners of the house are unconcerned; they keep the skull in a dedicated box and accept it as part of the house.

There are other stories around this noisy object, true, false and perhaps a mixture of both. One says that the slave and Pinney had a fight and when both men finished battering each other, the only fragment of either man was the skull; nobody knew whose skull it was. Another story states that in the 1960s an archaeologist named Michael Pinney owned Bettiscombe and he asked a pathologist to have a look at the skull. The pathologist proclaimed that the skull did not belong to a black male but to a local female who died between 1000 and 2000 BC. She was already in the area she belonged and may have been immersed in water for many hundreds of years. That brought out another theory that could be even more disturbing.

Long before Christianity, skulls were placed in prominent positions including being used as offerings to water spirits in sacred pools, rivers and wells. According to legend, people should treat these remains with care, even devotion and in return would protect the locals. So if the local population cares for the skull, it will return the favour.

There is yet another story connected to this screaming relic. According to legend, one house owner tried to rid the house of the curse of the skull by burying it. He dug a deep hole in the ground, placed the skull at the bottom and filled it back up. Slightly apprehensive, he went to bed, wondering if his sleep would be disturbed. He was not: the house was peaceful through the hours of darkness. Next morning he was in the garden to see the thing grinning at him from the top of the hole. Now that is a strange way for any self-respecting skull to behave. As far as I am aware, the skull remains in Bettiscombe.

Staying in the South, Bodmin Jail in Cornwall is said to have a scary number of ghosts. However bright the weather outside, the prison is a forbidding place with a dank and cheerless atmosphere that must have further depressed the feelings of the prisoners. The jail was built around 1779 and remained in use until the twentieth century. During that time at least sixty people were hanged here including Selina Wadge who threw her disabled son Harry into a well. Her ghost remains to plead for forgiveness from young children. There was also a hangman who made money on the side for cutting his execution ropes into fragments and selling the pieces to those who had a ghoulish nature. I wonder what happened to all the odd scraps of rope. Are they still sitting in attics and drawers the length and breadth of England, or has a succession of tidy wives long-since consigned them to the bin, where they belong? And that brings another possibility to mind: how many of the fragments were genuine and how many ghoulish collectors have hoarded lengths of rope that never saw a hanging and were only used to tie up a ship or a canal barge?

Selina Wadge may be the female ghost that walks around outside the jail while the people who work here have reported empty cells to have prisoners inside, staring out at them. The wandering woman may sometimes sneak into the jail, for children have claimed that a woman in the lower level has tried to grab them and then disappeared. Some of the cells have a shockingly oppressive atmosphere that depresses the spirits of even casual visitors.

Remaining in the south but moving eastward to Kent, there is the village of Pluckley, near Ashford, said to be the most haunted in all of England. There is no doubt that this picturesque village has its share of ghosts, with a Victorian lady, a weird light, a perforated highwayman and a wood haunted by unearthly screams. There is also a ghostly headmaster, surely the worst kind of nightmare for most school pupils. Living headmasters are bad enough for anybody.

As in many English villages, the church is as central to the community as it seems to be central to the local ghostly world. This church has a knocking sound at night, accompanied by a strange flickering light. Local legend claims that the light is a manifestation of Lady Dering who lived in the eleventh century.

That brings up some confusion, for there seem to be two ladies that haunt the area of St Nicholas's Church. One is red and the other white. According to one of the legends, the White Lady married Lord Dering, the landowner and they were much in love. When the lady died, her husband enclosed her in four separate coffins, one of oak and three of lead, so she retained her beauty and did not decompose.

Some accounts say similar things about the Red Lady. Others say the two were both ladies of the manor and may have been related, perhaps a mother and daughter or even sisters. It is unusual to have two spirits of different colours haunting the same house, but many strange things happen in England. The stories about the Red Lady have the addition that a red rose was lovingly placed in her coffin when she died, hence her different colouring. Where the accounts do agree, they say she is a sad ghost who searches the graveyard looking for her stillborn child.

There are many other ghosts in this spooky village. For instance, there is a phantom seventeenth-century highwayman who history has falsely named Robert DuBois. The legend places him on the road, and he had one *modus operandi*. DuBois used to hide behind a tree and jump out suddenly, then smack his shocked victims on the head. Because of his actions, this part of the village became known as Fright Corner, or sometimes Frith corner. DuBois eventually met his demise when some clever chap worked out the highwayman's routine and threw a spear that penetrated the tree and the highwayman. Using a spear as a weapon seems a bit old fashioned for the historical period, so perhaps there is a mixture of stories here, although some versions of the tale update the weapon to a more plausible sword. DuBois is still there in spirit, sometimes leaping out to frighten people, occasionally appearing with the spear or sword through his body. The name Frith may also mean peace or freedom, an expectation of hospitality and there is a possibility that people have misconstrued the name and have attached a false legend.

Perhaps DuBois is waiting for the phantom coach that also rattles through this most haunted of Kentish villages. People sometimes see this dark coach, and often only hear it as it clatters on Maltman's Hill. There seems no backstory for this vehicle, which is a pity.

And there is more. There is a ghostly monk at what used to be Rectory Cottage, together with a vague story that he had a very un-monkish affair with a lady from Rose Court. Naughty monk: perhaps his guilt keeps his spirit restless? The lady in question was rumoured to be another of the Dering clan. She still haunts Rose Court and committed suicide, perhaps because of her illicit affair. Her ghost keeps regular habits as she is seen between four and five in the afternoon as she takes her dogs for a walk.

Another tragic story surrounds the phantom colonel of Park Woods. Nobody knows anything about him although the legend says that he hanged himself in the woods and now appears in an officer's uniform. He is harmless, so do not be alarmed if you meet him.

Pluckley has other mysteries to offer. There is an old ruined windmill near the village. If one passes by and sees the dark silhouette of a man, then there is a storm coming. The ghost is reputed to be a gentleman by the name of Dicky Buss. That brings up another of the many suicides that seem to be so prevalent around this charming little village. Dicky Buss had a friend in Henry Turff, who was the headmaster of Smarden School. They used to meet regularly until one Sunday Turff disappeared on his way home from Buss's house. He was found hanging from a tree, and his ghost is sometimes seen in the area, dressed in striped trousers and a green blazer.

As if that spooky collection was not sufficient for one small village, there is also a ghost in the brickworks where a clay wall fell on a man, killing him, while an elderly lady haunts Pinnock Bridge. She sold watercress at the crossroads here, and one day she was smoking and drinking when a spark from her pipe set fire to her whisky, and she burned to death. She is still here, sometimes seen.

There is no point hiding from the ghosts in the local pubs, for the Black Horse has a poltergeist which shifts glasses and sometimes helps tidy up but also removes articles of clothing. A lady named Jessie Brooks is supposed to be the poltergeist, for she is also sometimes seen ghosting around the bar searching for a lost child. If that is not sufficient to tempt any spirit hunter into this pub, there is also something interesting that screams. Possibly he, she or it is hoping to be served, but not even the best barman can see an invisible spirit. A coachman, a cavalier and a young lady from the Tudor period haunt the one-time pub, the Blacksmith's Arms, now a private house. Once a hunting lodge, the nearby Dering Arms has a ghostly woman sitting at the bar, where she has been since before good Queen Victoria passed away.

Finally, for Pluckley there is a bush where people can dance around to summon the devil, should they wish to, and the Screaming Woods. Their real name is Dering Woods after the prominent local family, but if you happen to be here at night, you may hear the screaming of all the travellers who got lost in here. However, stories of a massacre in 1948 and students getting lost and never seen again have been proved to be hoaxes. All-in-all, Pluckley would seem to be a ghost hunter's Mecca and a nightmare for those people who have phasmophobia.

Even further south than Kent, the English Channel separates England from Continental Europe. It is undoubtedly one of the most historic stretches of water in the world and has seen Romans, Vikings, Crusaders, Elizabethan pirates and eighteenth-century privateers, smugglers, Nelson's navy and the invasion fleet for Normandy in 1944. As if that were not enough, there were also thousands of merchantmen and fishermen. It is not surprising that there are also nautical ghosts.

In 1878 the Bishop of Ripon was happily entertaining a guest when during the meal the visitor had a vision of a ship sinking in a sudden blizzard. At the same time, there was a squall off the Isle of Wight, and HMS *Eurydice* foundered with a terrible loss of life. Her master, Captain Marcus Hare, ordered every man to look after himself and went down with his ship, praying. Of her crew of three hundred and sixty-six, a schooner named *Emily* picked up five, of whom only two survived. A few months later *Eurydice* was raised and taken to pieces. Only the ship's bell now survives, hanging in Shanklin's St Paul's Church as a memorial to the dead.

Eurydice did not vanish forever. She has appeared since, again and again, sliding across the choppy seas to cause consternation and worry before vanishing again. Those who see her report the same thing, a three-masted vessel with her gun ports open. There is a story that sometime in the 1930s *Eurydice* sailed right in front of a submarine, which had to dive suddenly, only for the ship to disappear. Even more impressive in 1998 Prince Edward saw a sailing vessel appear and sail toward the spot where *Eurydice* had sunk. Then it disappeared. Apparently, there was no ship caught on radar.

Not long after the loss of *Eurydice*, there was another sea-related ghost recorded in England. On the 22nd June 1893, HMS *Victoria* was off the coast of Syria with Vice-Admiral Sir George Tryon in command. He ordered *Victoria* to alter course and steer toward HMS *Camperdown*, with whom she was in company. The manoeuvre was so obviously dangerous that Sir George's officers, including Lord Gillford, his flag lieutenant, protested, but Sir George did not listen. Admiral Tryon was renowned for ordering his officers to perform complex manoeuvres.

Eventually, as the two vessels closed with each other at some speed, Sir George came to his senses and ordered that they return to their original courses. By that time it was too late and the two ships collided. HMS *Victoria* blew up.

'It is all my fault,' Sir George said, quite correctly. These were his last words.

At the exact moment of his death, Sir George appeared in full naval uniform at his home in Eaton Square in London, where Lady Tryon was having a party. He walked across the room as if to bid a final farewell to his wife, and nobody ever saw him again. There were around a hundred guests at the party, and although some followed the admiral to say hello, nobody could find him. Others asked Lady Tryon why she had not told them her husband would be present; she had not expected him to call.

Another type of roving ghost is said to be frequently met on England's roads. These are the ghosts of the highwaymen, those supposedly romantic mounted thieves who infested the highways and byways. Dick Turpin, arguably the most celebrated of them all, still haunts Weathercock Lane in Aspley Guise, Bedfordshire. He is riding his horse, Black Bess, at great speed so either escaping pursuit or heading toward a coach packed with wealthy travellers. There is another ghost with highwayman associations at Lewtrenchard Manor near Oakhampton where the mother of a highwayman named Edward Gould guards the house. Unlike her wayward son, she is said to be friendly.

Although most highway robbers were male, an occasional female proved themselves as adept, skilful and dangerous as any of the men. One such woman was Lady Katherine Ferrers who lived between 1634 and 1660 and sometimes had a novel method of robbery. Rather than ride alongside her victim and point a pistol, she chose to climb up a tree that overhung a highway and drop on any unfortunate traveller who passed underneath. That was her unique but not her only method as she also shot at coachmen.

Lady Katherine, the original Wicked Lady, would change into her mask, breeches and tricorn hat in a secret room in her house and leave quietly, so her servants did not know about her other identity. She rode a black horse with white flashes on its forelegs so should have been quite conspicuous, or perhaps that was the idea; gain a reputation and the very sight of a highwaywoman may dishearten one's victims. Even apart from her thievery on the road, she seems to have been a lively and thoroughly unpleasant woman who was reputed to have burned down houses when the owners were still inside, killed a constable and shot cattle for the sheer fun of it.

This strangely unpleasant lady lived at Markyate Cell in Hitchin, Hertfordshire and her ghost is still there, pounding over the nearby Normansland Common on her distinctive horse or easing through the garden. She does not haunt the house itself although a later female ghost is there, ascending the stairs. Lady Ferrers is also reputed to have buried her loot under a tree near the house. Perhaps she is a lady best to avoid in death as she was in life.

In the village of Crondall in Hampshire, there is an Alma Lane that a messenger reputedly haunts. He was running to inform people about the Battle of Waterloo when a gang of footpads and highwaymen killed him. It is more than likely that the name of the lane has changed as the Battle of the Alma was not fought until 1854, nearly forty years after the victory at Waterloo. Apparently, there is also a flock of ghostly sheep in Crondall, which is strange.

Gloucestershire, that most lovely of counties has Snowshill Manor near Broadway, a house with a long and distinguished history and ghosts to match. The earliest record of Snowshill goes back to 821 AD when the King of Mercia gave the manor to Winchcombe Abbey, so this place predates the formation of England. It also has royal associations, as Henry VIII grabbed it, as he clutched so many places during the Dissolution of the Monasteries. Much later it was the home of a playful eccentric. Naturally, the fabric is much later than the old Mercian days with the earliest part of the building only dating to the late fifteenth century.

In 1919 an artist named Charles Paget Wade bought Snowshill and made it into a private museum for his lifetime's collection of objects from all around the world. Wade liked to show off his unusual assemblage while parading himself in a strange costume. He also dabbled a little in witchcraft, and related sciences. One room is still known as the Witch's Garret and has occult symbols on the walls, while some visitors claim that it has an eerie atmosphere.

Now the National Trust owns the property and all its contents including its ghosts, such as the Benedictine monk in the cowled cloak who drifts along the lane beside the house. There is also a frowning monk in the kitchen and another on the stairs; perhaps the same man or one of his colleagues; nobody has ever been able to decide.

The monk-haunted stairs lead to Ann's Room, which is also said to have its ghost, this time with a story attached. The Ann of the room is purported to be Ann Parsons who was only sixteen years old when she ran off with Anthony Palmer on the 13th February 1604. When they arrived at Snowshill Manor, the owner, Ann's uncle welcomed them in and whistled up a priest who married them there and then in Ann's Room in a rushed midnight service.

It was only unfortunate that Ann was already engaged to another man.

Presumably, that was the reason for Ann and Anthony's hurried departure from Snowshill for Chipping Campden. If they had hoped to escape, then they were mistaken for they ran straight into John Warne, Ann's angry guardian, and a bunch of his friends. Warne and his followers grabbed Ann but Anthony managed to free her, and they were soon on the run again. However, the Law caught up with them, and Anthony was charged with abduction and having an illicit marriage. Unfortunately even the most revealing legends do not give an outcome. We are left wondering what happened to Ann and Anthony.

Is the weeping girl in the green dress that haunts Ann's Room the ghost of Ann? Or is there another so-far untold story in that room? Ghost stories are intriguing, but they often leave a frustrating gap.

Other places in Snowshill are also haunted, with the Zenith Room sometimes resounding to the clatter of a blade on blade. This room was said to be the scene of a duel for whatever long-forgotten reason, but whether the story followed the sound of swordplay or the swords are a memory of that desperate day, nobody can tell.

There is at least one other named ghost, that of Charles Marshall who lived at Snowshill in the early decades of the nineteenth century. He appeared on numerous occasions after his 1858 death to inform a neighbouring farmer named Richard Carter about a secret hoard of money. Although Carter was initially terrified of the constant appearance of his dead companion, he followed instructions and showed Marshall's widow where she could find the money. She used the money to complete renovations of the house, or so the story says.

Finally, there are the ghostly footsteps that resound through the echoing rooms with their fascinating collection. People think that the steps are those of Charles Wade, touring his house, showing off his amazing artefacts and preparing to surprise his guests. That may well be so.

From the furthest north then, to the furthest south and all points in between, England is a land of ghosts. They are in public houses, churches and on the roads and even in the air. They can be frightening, sombre, sad or thought-provoking yet they are all part of the fascinating patchwork that makes up the strange country of England.

Chapter Two
The National Icon Who Never Existed

John Bull is to England what Uncle Sam is to the United States: a national personification. Arguably less well-known now than he once was, he is usually shown in the guise of an eighteenth-century farmer, prosperous and stout. Rather than sporting the English flag of Saint George he often wears a waistcoat emblazoned with the Union flag of Great Britain, thus heightening the confusion over flags and nationality that some people have.

Was there ever a real John Bull? There is no doubt that many thousands of men have sported the name John Bull, but one, in particular, stands out. John Bull (1562 – 1628) was a musician during the reign of Queen Elizabeth. He seems to have been a strange man who worked for the Virgin Queen before fleeing to the Netherlands pursued by predatory lawyers and angry husbands keenly wishing to discuss his alleged adultery with their wives.

What makes this particular John Bull interesting is the supposed fact that he was the composer of the tune *God Save the King* – or Queen. Is it strange that an adulterer should think up a melody that is known for its royal associations throughout the world?

Perhaps even more strangely, John Bull as a representation of England was the invention of a Scottish scientist and political satirist. John Arbuthnott lived from 1667 to 1735, so was thriving at the time of the Union of Parliaments in 1707. He depicted John Bull as a typical Englishmen, 'an honest, plain-dealing fellow, choleric, bold, and of a very inconstant temper.' The caricature struck a chord with the English, and by the 1760s John Bull was accepted as a representative figure of Englishness. At the time, stoutness and ruddy features were taken as a sign of healthy prosperity, while his low top hat has since earned the name of a John Bull topper. The bulldog at his side has also sometimes growled itself into acceptance as characteristically English.

In character, John Bull is a hard-headed countryman who likes his drink and his country sports, with no love for the intellectual. Is that true of English people today? Or was it only true of the English squirearchy of the eighteenth and nineteenth century? The John Bull figure perhaps gained its greatest popularity in the desperate days between 1793 and 1815 when England, in common with Scotland, Wales and Ireland, was engaged in a death-struggle with Revolutionary and Napoleonic France. During that period, people no longer viewed John Bull as a prosperous farmer, but as a symbol of English or even of British – hence the Union flag - defiance against the might of Napoleonic France.

As the nineteenth-century progressed, priorities altered. After the defeat of Napoleon Bonaparte, people's thoughts turned to political progress within the nation and an equal franchise. Once again John Bull became a symbol of stubborn refusal to back down. The character of this sturdy Englishman has been used to advertise goods and services thought to be most thoroughly English, with his bulldog and pugnacious attitude. Even yet, nearly three centuries after its creation, John Bull is thrust forward as a representation of the stubborn English. How strange that this English trademark should have been the brainchild of a Scotsman.

Chapter Three
The Love for Strange Sports and Games

England is undoubtedly the birthplace of Rugby. It was created at Rugby school in 1823 when a pupil named Webb Ellis picked up the ball and ran with it, rather than kicking it toward the opposition's goal. That is more folklore than fact, yet it is the official and the popular view so let's go along with it. Association Football, named soccer by some, may also have been invented in England, although Scotland has a strong claim.

There are other variations of football in England, including some whose history stretches back beyond ken. With names such as folk or mob football, these hectic encounters between rival villages had few rules and usually involved every male in the neighbourhood, all struggling to shift an inflated pig's bladder to some specified spot. Participants expected violence and mayhem in this pursuit of prestige for the town, and the odd broken bone or even broken neck only added to the day's fun.

Sanitised versions of the original continue in Alnwick in Northumberland, Ashbourne in Derbyshire, Atherstone in Warwickshire, Haxey in Lincolnshire and Workington in Cumbria. Each one has its charm and no doubt there are more.

Indeed there are many sporting traditions in England, including one of the most competitive leagues in world association football, an amazing prize-fighting and boxing history, blood sports such as fox-hunting and the now-illegal hare coursing, plus steeple-chasing, horse-racing, yachting and the ubiquitous and utterly English cricket. A favourite cricket anecdote comes from the Warborough Cricket Club in Oxfordshire who hopefully still play on the village green. This club has had its home in all of the five local pubs, and its motto is 'win or lose we enjoy our booze' – an excellent way to view things. What could be more English than sitting around a village green on a drowsy summer afternoon drinking beer or cider and watching men in white clothes battering a ball with a flat piece of wood?

Well, how about throwing Black Puddings? Now that is a strange sport. Merrie England was not always so merry, or so peaceful. In the fifteenth century, the country was ripped apart by a bitter civil war that flared up and down the country for decades of pointless slaughter. Being English, it has been given the name Wars of the Roses, as if to sanitise the blood and agony although the Scottish novelist, Sir Walter Scott, was responsible for popularising that particular term.

To summarise what was a complex series of events, it was a dynastic struggle for the English throne, with two branches of the Plantagenets vying for supremacy.

One side was the House of York, whose symbol, according to tradition, was a white rose and the other was the House of Lancaster, who, again according to tradition, preferred red roses. After initial ugly bickering, the war proper started in 1455 and continued with breaks for recuperation and no-doubt refreshment until 1487. Despite the many horrific incidents and atrocities during this period, there seems no after-taste of bitterness. As a matter of interest, Henry Tudor, Earl of Richmond won the war for the Red Rose of Lancaster when he defeated King Richard III at Bosworth Field. He became Henry VII and to show there was no ill-feeling he married Elizabeth of York. The Tudors then ruled England until Queen Elizabeth died and the Scottish Stuarts took the throne.

Much more important is the effect that long-gone war had on the strange traditions of English sport. According to legend, at the Battle of Stubbins Bridge in Lancashire in 1455, the armies of York and Lancaster met each other once again. They fired off all their ammunition and wondered what to do next. It seems that neither army was particularly blood-thirsty that day as rather than resort to swords and spears they lifted their food supplies and pelted one another instead. The Lancashire men used black puddings and the Yorkshire men Yorkshire puddings. It must have been a messy if bloodless battle.

Today that battle is re-enacted in the World Black Pudding Throwing Championship as rivals meet in the Lancashire town of Ramsbottom each year to see who is better at tossing black puddings. The organisers place a pile of twelve giant Yorkshire puddings on a plinth twenty feet high, and the competitors must throw black puddings at them. Only underarm throws are allowed, and the winner is the man or woman who can knock most down. Now that sounds like strange fun.

Unfortunately for the legend, the Wars of the Roses were not exclusively between Yorkshire and Lancashire. Those who participated knew it as the War of the Cousins, and they did not fight under any colour of rose. One faction fought beneath a red dragon and the other under the sign of a white boar. The House of Lancaster recruited from all over north England, and Yorkshire men came from the south, or Wales or even Ireland. The rose idea came from Shakespeare's *Henry VI part 1* when the rival sides plucked roses from the Temple Garden to prove their respective loyalty. Perhaps there was some cynicism in Shakespeare's words for at his time 'to pluck a rose' was slang for relieving oneself.

There is also a spoil-sport story that the incident at Stubbins Bridge did not take place at all and the black pudding throwing did not begin until 1839 when mill workers from the rival counties had a competition in the town. The competition revived in 1984 and now attracts quite a crowd. Who cares about historical reality? It is fun, and it is strange: what more does one need?

The fist-sized black puddings are wrapped in women's tights to give a better grip, each competitor has only three shots, and when the spectators weary of watching food hurling through the air they can always retire to the nearby pub. Sensibly, there is usually a public house connected to most English sports. Some people may wonder what a Lancashire black pudding is: well it's a concoction of oats and onions mixed with pig's blood. It may sound strange, but it is delicious. For those who are interested, Yorkshire puddings are much lighter and are made of flour, eggs and milk.

But who won the original battle of Stubbins Bridge? Apparently, the raiding Yorkshire men could not stand against the hail of black puddings and ran back over the border.

However, if throwing black puddings does not appeal, how would you fancy cheering on your favourite snail over the World Snail Racing Championships? This competition is held annually in Congham, Norfolkshire. Apparently, the common garden snail makes the headlines here as they speed over the course toward the finishing line. There are heats throughout racing day and a grand final where the speediest snails line up side by side on a damp cloth and charge along a circular track for a massive thirteen inches – that's about 32 centimetres for those of a metric persuasion.

It was a man named Tom Elwes who brought the World Championship to Congham sometime in the 1960s after being excited by a similar race in France. With a low altitude and damp climate, Congham is ideal snail territory so the little creatures will feel right at home with no need for altitude adjustment before proving their paces on the track. Some of the snails are impressively speedy with one hero with the name of Archie clocking up a time of two minutes to complete the course. At the time of writing, Archie holds the world record in a World Championship competition that can attract as many as two hundred snails every year, with spectators standing by, cheering for their favourite.

Is there a prize? Of course, there is. The winning snail and World Champion gains a silver tankard, for which he or she may not have much use, but the lettuce leaves inside are sure to be appreciated. And in case anybody thinks that snail racing is just a waste of time, any money raised goes toward keeping the thirteenth-century St Andrew's Church in good repair. Not many churches can claim snails as benefactors.

Surrey hosts the UK Wife-Carrying championship, where dedicated husbands heft their ever-beloved over three hundred metres of rough ground. Although the *Daily Mail* has termed it Non-PC (which could be an encouragement to compete), the organisers laughed that off. The winner is said to receive a barrel of local ale, while the loser has the consolation prize of a tin of dog food. Is there some symbolism in that award? The man in the dog-house perhaps?

One sport that is very specific to place and time is Hunting the Mallard. This game, known as the Gaudy, is restricted to All Souls College in Oxford on Mallard Day. There is no element of animal cruelty here for the quarry is a giant mallard that apparently erupted from a drain when the foundations were built in 1437. A student known as the Chief Mallard leads the hunters, each of whom carries a long stick and a mallard medal. This sport caused so much disruption that it is rarely held now – perhaps once a century.

Another sport that reaches its apogee in England is Pooh-stick racing. Now if you have never read A. A. Milne's books about Winnie the Pooh, specifically the *House at Pooh Corner* you may not understand this game. Milne was an author who had survived the horrors of the First World War and created characters such as Winnie the Pooh, Eeyore and Christopher Robin. With their gentle prose and theme of constant friendship, his books are an antidote to the nightmare of the trenches.

Pooh-Stick racing is a perfect family game for a summer afternoon. First one and one's friends or children find a bridge over a gentle stream, then one selects sticks of roughly equal size and drop them over the parapet of the bridge, all together. The sticks must fall and not be thrown, which is a serious offence and makes the competitor liable to instant disqualification. Either the oldest or youngest person must start the game by dropping the first stick.

The second the competitors release their sticks, they will saunter to the opposite side of the bridge to see them emerge. The person whose stick is first to appear is the winner. It is a simple, cheery little game that every lover should play with their partner and every parent with his or her children.

The World Pooh-Sticks-Championship was held at Little Wittenham, Oxfordshire for many years until it grew so popular that there was insufficient parking for the number of competitors' and spectators' vehicles. For over thirty years the Rotary Club of Oxford Spires had organised the event with the River Thames as the waterway concerned and Day's Lock as the venue. There was panic in the Pooh-Stick fraternity when the organisers announced that they had to find a new venue. The stick droppers searched for a new stretch of river along which to race, Pooh-lovers scanned maps and charts, and river-owners wondered if their particular stretch of water was good enough to be honoured. Fear turned to relief when they located a new arena.

A common between Witney and Cogges Manor Farm in West Oxfordshire was the new site of the World Pooh-Sticks championship and a better location would be hard to find. With an evocative and very English name like the Windrush River on which to float the sticks and around seven hundred people turning up to compete, the world championships seem assured of a smiling future.

Now: where is my Pooh Stick?

Marsden in West Yorkshire holds an annual Cuckoo Festival that celebrates the return of that legendary bird from warmer climates. There is a local story that the villagers once tried to prevent the bird from migrating by encasing it in a tower, but the bird flew away just as the builders placed the final stones. Anybody who has lived near a calling cuckoo may agree that their persistent monotonous call can grate on the nerves, though.

The next game was once so familiar that every boy and many girls played it every autumn without fail. Conkers. How many school playgrounds resounded with the cheery smack of horse-chestnut on horse-chestnut? Probably thousands and now the World Conker Championships are held in England, the nation that invented the game.

There is no way of knowing for how long children have bored holes in the shining fruit of the horse chestnut tree, strung a cord through and battered hell out of their best friend's conker to be a one-er. As the competitor defeated more of his or her opponents, so the conker's number grew – a two-er, a three-er and so on until it was a chipped champion veteran of the conker season and possibly allowed to go into honourable retirement.

Whatever happened in the unknown past, the first recorded conker battle took place in 1848, the Year of Revolutions throughout Europe and the Year of Conkerers in England. The Isle of Wight was the venue and what could be more English than that little triangular island off the south coast? However, it was not until 1965 that the official World Conker Championship started at Ashton in Northamptonshire, on a village green in the shadow of spreading horse chestnut trees, as was right and proper.

The beginning of this major sporting event was inauspicious with a few local men playing each other and giving money to charity. A game that started as a one-off became a regular fixture, with outsiders entering the village to challenge the indigenous conkerers. The organisers sent any profit to the Royal National Institute for the Blind for Talking Books. Gradually news spread outside Northamptonshire and even outside England until in 1976 Jorge Ramirez, a Mexican national, became Conkerer of the world. Females can also participate of course, with overseas ladies as welcome as juniors. Now held at Southwick in Northamptonshire, the World Conker Championships are a fixture in the English sporting calendar.

In my day, far too many years ago, playing conkers was common all through autumn. I believe that some schools have banned them now for apparent health and safety concerns. If anything should encourage conkers, then an unimaginative and politically correct blanket ban should. The rules are simple, as the best rules should be. Each player had three whacks at his opponent's conker, attempting to smash it to pieces, and then the opponent has his or her revenge. There were various methods of helping victory, such as baking the conker or even – cheating – by adding illegal substances such as glue inside the small hole where the string penetrated the conker. One could also soak the conker in vinegar, paraffin or salt water or even paint it with nail varnish. More legally, the top part of the conker is the hardest; if the striker can manipulate this area to hit hard against the weaker sides of the opponent, then he or she is closer to victory.

Conkers is a simple game, very satisfying to smack one's conker against that of an opponent but only in England would there be a world championship.

Much more painful sounding and many times more strange is the World Stinging Nettle Championship. Nettles can pack a powerful sting, but if you fancy eating your way through scores of two-foot-long nettle-stalks, then Marshwood in Dorset is the place to go. The venue, as one would expect in England, is the village pub, the perfectly named Bottle Inn and dozens of people volunteer to chomp their way through a pile of stingers. The pub is so named because it was the first in the area to sell bottled beers: that's another piece of strange history.

There are good reasons to keep nettles in the garden or farm for people can make nettle soup, nettle beer and nettle tea. They are high in vitamin C so combat scurvy as well as purifying the blood. As we all know, they also pack a healthy sting. Apparently, they are not native to England, with the Romans given credit for introducing them to Britannia for self-flagellation and other strange practices that I for one would not recommend. The theory was that the Romans used the plant to keep warm in winter, which is unlikely as nettles flourish in summer and die back in the cold months. In saying that, seventeenth-century herbals convinced their readers that nettles helped the brain and the senses, cured insomnia, restored hair to the bald, eased the sting of burns and chilblains and protected against witchcraft. If one looks closely into a patch of nettles, it may be possible to see the fairies that are said to live there, which is another excellent reason to allow this plant to remain in one's garden.

So nettles are definitely worth a second look. In some places, they were known as the 'naughty man's plaything' with the 'naughty man' being another term for the devil. Enough theory: what about the game?

Unlike many other sports, nettle-eating does not have a long history. It seems that it started as recently as 1997 when two Dorset farmers argued about who had the longest nettles, with the loser having to eat a stem. The rules now are simple: how many lengths of nettle can you put away in one hour of continual eating. Apparently, the competitors hardly notice the sting of the nettles but do suffer from a black tongue and aching jaws with the constant chewing, although the cheering of the crowd may help alleviate the pain. When the competitors eat the leaves, judges measure the bare stalks to see who has eaten the most. The current record stands at an impressive eighty feet of stalk. Any takers? Don't all rush at once, now!

There is a different kind of pain during the World Coal Carrying Championships that take place at Gawthorpe in West Yorkshire. This is not a single event but a number of different competitions, with a men's race, a women's, children's and seniors, with varying weights of coal to carry uphill. Not surprisingly, pubs also feature in these events.

The Men's Veterans Race kicks off the day; then the women show their strength and endurance, followed by the original and main men's event. The women carry 20 kilograms of coal – slightly under half a hundredweight - and the men fifty kilograms – about a hundredweight. The race starts outside the Royal Oak pub - locally known as the Barracks - in Owl Lane in Ossett and extends a tough 1108 yards to the Maypole in the Village Green in Gawthorpe. The children run a shorter course of 150 or so yards. At the time of writing the world record holder is David Jones of Meltham with a time of four minutes and six seconds. The women's record holder is Catherine Foley in a time of four minutes 25 seconds.

Now the most obvious question is: why? Why would men and women want to carry a massive bag of coal for nearly a mile at speed? It all started back in time, or rather in 1963 at the Beehive Inn in Gawthorpe. Two men, Reggie Sedgewick and Amos Clapham, were at the bar having a quiet pint or two. A third man named Lewis Hartley crashed into the bar and said he thought that Reggie looked extremely tired – or 'buggered' in the local parlance. He accompanied the words with a hefty slap on the back that nearly floored the unprepared Reggie.

Slightly irritated by the accusation and the slap, Reggie claimed he was as fit as Lewis and challenged him to a race carrying a bag of coal. The idea appealed and grew into a local event and then into the grandly named World Championships.

Tetbury in the Cotswolds has a similar weight-lugging ordeal with the Woolsack Races where competitors hoist sacks of wool on their shoulders and run or stagger two hundred and forty tough yards between two pubs, The

Crown and the Royal Oak. The Cotswolds was always excellent sheep-raising country, so a wool sack race here makes perfect sense.

A gentler world championship is held each year at Mytholmroyd, by Hebden Bridge in Yorkshire's Calder Valley. This competition is the World Dock Pudding Championship, where the best Dock Pudding is sought, cooked and eaten. Now, in case you have not tried this local delicacy, so here is a brief list of the ingredients: dock leaves, oatmeal, nettles, onions, butter and seasoning. It sounds like a very healthy dish for the pure vegetarian. Apparently, there is a specific kind of dock leaf used, the *Polygonum Bistorta*, which is sweeter than the common or garden cow dock leaves. In some cases, the dock pudding forms part of breakfast. There is a story that during the Second World War Lord Haw Haw, the traitor who spouted false propaganda for Nazi Germany, claimed that food rationing had driven Yorkshire people to eat grass. If he had tried a healthy Dock Pudding, perhaps he would have realised that his monstrous regime had no chance of winning the war against the folk of Yorkshire. 'Aye up, Adolf, that's a threp in't steans for you.'

When it began in 1971, the first World Dock Pudding Championship received national television coverage and quite right too. It is only strange that more people do not try this unique Yorkshire delicacy.

Once fed on healthy Yorkshire fare, why not nip down to Devon for a spot of that traditional old English pastime of worm charming? If you don't wish to travel as far as Devon, Cheshire has a rival World Worm Charming Championship. Both have slightly different rules, but the result is the same: bring earthworms to the surface.

The Devon championships are held in Blackawton and have been since 1983.

As so often in England, it all started in a pub. It was in 1983 when two men were drinking copiously in the Normandy Arms in Blackawton. One of these thirsty gentlemen was later winding his way home and stopped in a field to answer the call of nature. The flow of liquid attracted worms to the surface and the gentleman in question casually wondered if he could found an annual worm-charming event. In 1984 the competition started and never looked back. People seemed intrigued by the skills needed to charm worms and the numbers involved increased. Today it is a major event in the local sporting calendar.

The Cheshire event began slightly earlier, with a local man, Tom Shufflebotham, showing his skill in July 1980 when he enticed over five hundred worms to the surface within half an hour. That was the beginning of an annual competition held at the same Cheshire village with eighteen strict if tongue-in-cheek rules and a stern committee to ensure that nobody cheats. Indeed there is an International Federation of Charming Worms and Allied Pastimes in place, which also overlooks other major sporting events such as underwater Ludo and ice tiddly-winks. Only in England...

Horse racing is probably as old as horse riding, but commercial horse racing with fixed courses and dates seems to be a relatively new idea. Said to be the oldest flat race in England, the Kiplingcotes Derby must also be the most unusual. It began in 1519 and takes place on the third Thursday in March, whatever the weather. It is a strange course for a flat race, with the four-mile route climbing nearly three hundred feet as it crosses fields, a railway bridge and a road. Sufficient hazards there for any purist.

There are a few differences between this and other races. For a start men and women compete in total equality, and all have to weigh more than ten stones. If there are lightweights who do not meet this criterion, then they are permitted to carry heavy objects to make up the weight, with the stipulation that they cannot jettison them en-route and thus give their horses an unfair advantage. However, the rules also state that riders cannot hinder or even attack a rival entrant, which must be a comfort in fiercely-competitive England.

A fortunate clerk earns the princely sum of twenty-five pence every year for ensuring the course is in good condition, and the race takes place near Market Weighton in Yorkshire. The race is open to anybody who gathers at the sandstone starting post by eleven in the morning. The £50 winner's prize may not seem huge by today's standards, but people flock here to take part. One rule states that if the race is ever not run, then it has to stop forever. To ensure continuity, during the great snow of 1947 a lone farmer led his horse the length of the course, something that was repeated when foot and mouth disease hit the country in 2001.

These are only some of the strange events that grace the English sporting calendar. There is also Mangold hurling on Sherston, Gloucestershire, the Biggest Liar in the World Competition at Santon Bridge, Cumbria – so be careful of all the world's politicians gathering here – the Plank-Walking Championships at Queensborough, Kent, and the World Gurning Championship in Egremont in Cumbria.

Gurning is the art of making ugly faces, in case you were unsure. No make-up is allowed, although those competitors who wear false teeth are permitted, even encouraged, to rock, rattle and roll them at the audience if that helps make them more ugly than nature intended. The championships take place at the local Crab Fair, which started around 1267 when the Lord of the Manor handed out crab-apples to the locals. Perhaps that is why they gurned. Other sports at the Fair include a pipe-smoking competition.

There is more- a Pea shooting championship at Ely and Pea Throwing at Lewes, East Sussex, the Cooper's Hill Cheese-Rolling- and Wake in Gloucestershire, Welly-Wanging in Yorkshire and Egg-jarping at Peterlee, County Durham... England seems to be the home of strange sports, where participation and having fun is more important than pocketing a cheque for winning.

Other sports had a much darker side. Landowners and their guests liked to kill what was known as game, which was often deer or birds such as pheasant or grouse. The elite preserved these animals for sport, with gamekeepers responsible for ensuring sufficient of them survived the attention of poachers to be available for the legal owners to slaughter. In the eighteenth and nineteenth-century, rural England was the scene of virtual warfare. Gangs of poachers battled the gamekeeper and his men, who retaliated with spring-guns, booby traps and man-traps with serrated teeth that could permanently maim anybody they snapped shut on.

Naturally, all this intense sporting rivalry attracted its share of sporting eccentrics, many of whom practised their strangeness while astride a horse. England was the home of fox-hunting, where packs of men and women in red jackets chased after foxes, cornered them and watched as packs of hounds ripped them to shreds. That in itself is strange, but foxhunting became a way of life for some, a reason for existing and spawned such songs as *D'ye Ken John Peel?* The John Peel in question may have been Sir Frederick Fletcher Vane, a Cumberland man who wore a grey coat and could ride fifty miles a day in pursuit of the uneatable fox. As always, there are other versions of the story and other claimants for the main character, but the story of a man who lived to hunt remains the same. The Border Regiment marched to John Peel's tune throughout their long and distinguished history so making John Peel kent from Burma to Dunkirk and Shanghai to Ireland.

One other version says that the hunter's name was, in fact, John Peel and he lived in Cumbria, married Mary White in 1797 and hunted foxes, pine martens and hares. He was also said to have died in 1854 due to a hunting accident: the best way for a keen huntsman to go. According to legend, three landlords named their inns in honour of Peel's hounds: the Hark to Bounty at Slaidburn, the Towler at Bury and the Bellman at Clitheroe. The latter was named after a pure white hound, a strange colour for a hunting dog. It is once again noticeable how often pubs and sports coexist in England.

Often young sportsmen combined sport with heavy gambling and womanising. These were the 'plungers', 'bucks' and 'bloods' who feature in so many Regency romances. The reality would make the fictional stories pale into shocked insignificance, yet some of these bucks were also talented and brave sportsmen whose exploits would make today's highly-paid stars wince. For example, Sir Tatton Sykes of Sledmere in Yorkshire never missed the St Ledger race meeting for seventy-four consecutive years and once raced from Yorkshire to Aberdeen and back. Or there was Henry Chaplin who hunted six days a week, kept four packs of hounds and rewarded his trainer with £5,000 when his horse won the 1867 Derby. He died broke as a result of his lavish lifestyle.

Most outstanding was probably the Squire of All England, Squire Osbaldeston (1786 – 1866). Osbaldeston was a Yorkshire man who inherited money early and whose mother was perhaps too indulgent, he was expelled from Eton and just scraped through Oxford. He sniffed at politics and in those pre-Reform days became Whig MP for East Retford but found the whole parliamentary procedure a 'great bore'. He was also a fine cricketer, oarsman and played tennis like a Wimbledon champion. Naturally, he was also an excellent horseman and gambled on his skill. On one occasion he wore out twenty-eight horses riding two hundred miles in nine hours on Newmarket racecourse and then rode home for dinner with his friends. As usual, he was riding for a bet. When he was aged sixty-eight, Squire Osbaldeston came a creditable second in a Goodwood horse race.

Sport, gambling and women dominated the Squire's life. Good with bat and ball he played cricket for Surrey, Sussex and Middlesex, with single wicket matches being a bit of a speciality as long as there was a sizeable bet attached. Osbaldeston was a crack shot, able to dispose of one hundred pheasants with the same number of balls, and who could extract the ace of diamonds from a pack of cards, step back thirty feet and fire ten shots from a duelling pistol with each one perforating the card. However, when he participated in a duel on Wormwood Scrubs with Lord George Bentinck, who had welshed on a bet and accused him of cheating, both parties missed their mark. Contemporary accounts said that the participants or their seconds rigged the affair, so there was no bloodshed: duelling was illegal, and a fatal duel could carry the death penalty.

The Squire hunted, of course, trying out every famous hunting area in turn and once being bitten by a hound that he suspected had rabies. Despite his undoubted sporting talent, Osbaldeston does not seem to have been an attractive man; he had a quick temper that led to many disputes. However successful a sportsman, he was not lucky with the ladies, having a string of affairs and being suspected of fathering the odd illegitimate child but without finding a partner who was willing to cope with his excesses. He pursued women as avidly as foxes, with stories of one particular ball where he slept with both the host's daughters one after the other. He did not marry until he was 65, and even then it was for money. His gambling and hunting had reduced his fortune, so he had to sell his estate. He spent the final years of his life in his wife's house in Regent's Park, which must have been a drab sort of life for such an active man.

So there we have it, a selection of strange English sports and games, and a couple of the interesting people who enhanced or at least intensified the lives of all who met them. The next chapter will introduce some more eccentrics, and we will enter many more public houses and inns deeper into the book.

Chapter Four
A Talent for Eccentricity

One thing that England has always produced is eccentrics. It seems that the English have an obsession for parading people who are wired differently from the pack, or who refuse to accept conformity as a way of life. And quite right, of course. The world would be a drab, grey place if everybody followed contemporary trends, wore the same clothes and strove only to fit in. However, some people can go just a little too far in their desire to be different.

Real eccentrics require wealth, and freedom to express themselves, which is presumably why so many eccentrics come from the upper echelons of society.

One such was the fifth Duke of Portland, or William John Cavendish Scott Bentick to give him his full name. Like many people, he was a bit shy, but unlike others, he had the means to do something about it. While the poor just have to face their fears day-by-day, a duke could use his wealth and position to avoid anybody he wished to.

In the case of the Duke of Portland, that meant shunning just about everybody.

The duke's first step was to ban people from visiting Welbeck Abbey, his Nottinghamshire home. His next was to carve out a new domain under the ground. Not just a cellar, for he had miles of tunnels joining his underground billiard room and ballroom to the other chambers and from his coach house to the railway station at Worksop. The duke lined the tunnels with oak, painted them pink and filled them with boxes packed with wigs. Why the wigs and the pink? You would have to ask the duke that; nobody else knew.

There was also an underground observatory, which seems a bit of an oxymoron until you learn it had a glass roof, and there was a ballroom with a ceiling painted like a sunset. Naturally, the reticent duke did not have any actual balls in this room; that would mean inviting people.

Money talks, so the duke had his private railway carriage, complete with blacked-out windows, driven underground for over a mile to the nearest railway station, where busy workers loaded it onto a train. On arrival in London, he had his coachman drive to his townhouse in Cavendish Square, where he disembarked in secrecy and retreated to his study. The duke had other foibles such as giving his servants donkeys to ride to work and umbrellas to shelter them from the fierce English sun. He also had a roller-skating rink built but forbade any servant from talking to him on pain of instant dismissal. Only his valet was allowed any personal contact.

At one time the duke was relatively rational, but as he grew more eccentric with every passing year. When he did leave his mansion, it was usually by night with a female servant walking in front with a lantern held aloft, to either light the way or warn others away. On the rare occasions the duke ventured out by day, he hid behind a huge umbrella, two coats with high collars and an over-high top hat. He seemed to like the taste of chicken for he always had one roasting and his servants sent his food on trucks that ran through his tunnel network.

The duke had not always been so reluctant to meet people. He had spent years in the army, rising to the rank of Captain, and then entering politics, where his lethargy insured that he did nothing of note. However, he had managed to father three illegitimate children, which argues for some personal activity.

The reticent duke died at Harcourt House in London, and the curious could, at last, see the conditions in which he lived. He had stripped the interior of the house of furniture except for a few rooms in one wing, and even here there was the bare minimum. He had all the other rooms in the house painted bright pink. The pink-loving, tunnel travelling duke is long gone now, but people still remember his eccentric behaviour.

Dr John Dee was another strange old fellow. He liked to dabble in magic and moonlighted as an agent of the government when he had the time. He lived in the sixteenth century, and his good friend Edward Kelley claimed the ability to speak to spirits. When one of these spirits ordered Kelley to become intimate with the less-than-reluctant Mrs Dee, the good Doctor could only agree. Mrs Dee, Jane Fromond, had been twenty-one when she married Dee, who was thirty years her senior. Jane was his third wife and perhaps significantly, the only one to bear his children, or maybe Kelley's children.

Probably more important than his neglect of his wife's affairs, Dr Dee collected hundreds of books and tried to found an English national library, but those in authority rejected this novel idea. In August 1560 Dr Dee used his powers in the churchyard at Walton-le-Dale in Lancashire where a rich corpse had unsportingly refused to divulge the whereabouts of his fortune. According to legend, Dr Dee revived the body and found out the location. He is remembered for his science as much as his occult practices at a time that the two were beginning to separate.

While the Duke of Portland chose to live underground and Dr Dee lived on the fringes of science and magic, Lord Rokeby of Mount Morris near Hythe preferred to live in water. He was so fond of water that he built a glass topped tank beside his house, filled it with water and remained inside with his huge beard floating on the surface and his servants bringing him meals in the tank. On odd occasions Rokeby would leave the tank, travel to the beach and soak there instead, often having to be hauled ashore. When not floating or swimming in the water he would drink it, but the practice did him no harm at all.

Lord North preferred hibernation to floating. He retired to his bed on the 9th October and did not emerge until 22nd of March, every year. That was the family's unique method of atoning for a previous Lord North's part in losing the American colonies. Despite his strange habits, Lord North was no recluse but entertained people in his bedroom, with a twenty-five foot long dining table sharing his room. His American wife, apparently, was most surprised.

She would have been even more surprised if she had married Francis Henry Egerton (1756 – 1829), the eighth Earl of Bridgewater. At least Lord North had human beings ranged around his table. The Earl of Bridgewater preferred dogs, a dozen at a time and each with its little white napkin, personal servant and silver dishes. The earl did not like women and thought even gentlemen were too badly behaved to share his table.

The Earl's favourite dogs were named Biche and Bijou, until one day they broke his behavioural code and acted in a very doggy-like manner.

'These blackguards have deceived me,' the earl complained to his tailor. 'I have treated them like gentlemen, they have behaved like rascals. Take their measure! They shall wear for eight days the yellow coats and knee breeches of my valets, and stay in the anteroom, and be deprived of the honour of seeing me for a week.'

When they behaved, the earl treated his dogs to handmade boots and allowed them to use his carriages whenever they wished. Despite this glaring idiosyncrasy, the earl was highly intelligent, a scholar and a translator who collected manuscripts. Educated at Oxford, he was a Fellow of the Royal Society and a Fellow of the Society of Antiquities. He was also rumoured to have outfaced Napoleon Bonaparte when that gentleman wished to destroy his Paris home. To return to his eccentricities: when not feeding his dogs, the earl could admire his collection of boots. He was one pair every day and liked to display them around the room. And why not?

Other eccentrics were more locally famous, such as J. S. W. Erle-Drax. Outside Kent, it is unlikely if anybody remembers the Mad Major Erle-Drax yet in his day he was a locally prominent man. His statue is on the grounds of Olantigh, on the outskirts of Wye village. He was a local man although his wealth came from a fortunate marriage. He served in the East Kent Volunteers, was MP for Wareham in Dorset and dressed his hunt in orange and black rather than the more traditional red. Erle-Drax thought nothing of riding his horse across the railway line, so the train had to stop. Yet it was his obsession with his death and funeral that caused people to remember him

He rehearsed his funeral, following the cortege as it carried his coffin, with a model of himself carefully installed, along the route he had chosen. Perhaps the workers on his estate thought the whole idea was a bit absurd, and certainly they did not know he was following, for once out of direct line of sight of the house they dumped the coffin in the lee of a yew hedge and scarpered.

Concerned in case that should happen during his real funeral, Erle-Drax retained his coffin, having it beside his bedroom door in case of sudden death. It was there for around twenty years. There is no record of his funeral cortege casting aside the genuine coffin.

There is another funeral story from Kent, where a man named Darnell was buried in 1720. As the mourners gathered around his grave and the coffin was lowered, a man in a dark cloak was watching avidly.

'That is me they are burying' he said and slipped away. For some reason, the grave was re-opened years later, and Darnell's coffin was found to be open and filled with stones. Nobody ever discovered why, or what happened to the man in the dark cloak.

Then there was Simeon Ellerton, the stone man. There have been peoples and individuals throughout history who were obsessed with fitness. The ancient Spartans were proud of their hardihood for example, and some Englishmen. One of these men was Simeon Ellerton who lived through the eighteenth century.

If he had been born a century later he would have been known as a follower of pedestrianism- he liked to walk. The walk for which he is most noted was from Durham to London, but he also walked shorter distances as a volunteer courier or to oblige his friends. As he walked, Ellerton collected stones and carried them in a bag on his head. It may have been eccentricity, but there was reason behind the madness for he hoped to build himself a house.

It seems he did so, ending with a small stone cottage but the habit stuck and Ellerton continued to collect stones all his life, walking the rocky roads with a bag on his head.

Sometimes the eccentricity of tha aristocracy reached international proportions. Edward Hyde, Lord Cornbury, the third Earl of Clarendon, could have created a major incident because of the manner in which he liked to dress. At the beginning of the eighteenth century, Queen Ann sent him across the Atlantic to bc Governor of the Colony of New York and Jersey. He had no choice, even although he was her cousin. In fact, he carried his position a little too far. Deciding that he should make it obvious that the monarch he represented was a woman, he dressed in female attire. When the New York Assembly gathered in 1702, Lord Cornbury wore a full woman's gown, satin shoes and a fancy fan. One wonders what the

New Yorkers made of their new governor as he continued with his cross-dressing. He bought only the best hooped silk gowns, leaving himself short of money for anything else, even for clothing his wife, who must have wondered what sort of man she had married. With the unfortunate Lady Cornbury having to steal clothes for herself, Lord Cornbury was summoned back to England in 1708. He continued to wear women's clothing.

Or so the story goes.

The reality may be less colourful and more unsavoury. Graduating from Oxford, the then Viscount Cornbury joined the Royal Regiment of Dragoons and was the Tory Member of Parliament for Wiltshire between 1685 and 1696 and later for Christchurch. Although he was a Page of Honour at the coronation of King James VII and II, when William and Mary staged the Glorious Revolution, Cornbury was quick to desert the Stuarts with his dragoons.

That same year of 1688 he secretly married Lady Katherine O'Brien. It was 1701 that Cornbury became Governor of New York and New Jersey, a position he held for seven years. He colonists despised him, apparently while the historian Lord Macauley thought him a man of 'slender abilities, loose principles, and violent temper.' People also called him the 'worst governor Britain ever imposed on an American colony'. While taking bribes seems to have been the norm for politicians at the time, Cornbury was excessive and also robbed the treasury for his personal use. It is during this period that his reputation for wearing women's clothes began and there is said to be a portrait of him so attired, with the legend: 'unknown woman' attached.

With a preference to be known as 'His High Mightiness', it was said that Lord Cornbury attended the funeral of his wife dressed as a woman. Recalled from the Colonies, he was immediately imprisoned for debt and only released on his father's death when he became the 3rd Earl of Clarendon. He was still in debt when he died in 1732.

If such a man was typical of the governors that Britain sent over to the Colonies, is it surprising that they rebelled in the 1770s? The only strange thing is that they waited so long.

William Beckford was no Lord Cornbury. Instead, William Beckford was a builder. When he was aged ten, in 1770, he became heir to a million pounds – worth many times more than that in today's money, as well as lucrative plantations in Jamaica. That would make him an immensely wealthy little boy. At a time when the average working man would be lucky to earn fifty pounds a year, William Beckford would pocket £100,000.

Perhaps not sure what to do with such an immense amount of money, Beckford began to build. He liked buildings with towers, and he wanted them erected there and then, without waiting. Beckford owned the Fonthill Estate in the pleasant land of Wiltshire and in 1794 he hired five hundred men to build a Gothic abbey. He fed them beer and spurred them on with encouraging shouts and useless advice.

Rather than wait for deep foundations, the impatient Beckford had his men build them shallower, yet was surprised, six years later when his three hundred foot high spire fell during a gale. While most men may have despaired at the destruction of their creation, Beckford merely ordered his workforce to start on a new one; after all, he could afford it. That abbey took seven years to build. His abbey, built at such expense, did not last long but at least the building of it provided employment.

He had other minor foibles as well as building magnificent follies. Like so many English eccentrics, Beckford had strange living habits. Unmarried, his only close companion in his abbey was a tiny Spaniard, although every day he had his table set for a dozen people.

Lionel Walter Rothschild was another man born into great wealth. He was the eldest son of Emma Louise von Rothschild and Nathan Rothschild, 1st Baron Rothschild, wealthy banker and England's first ever Jewish peer. Walter, as he was known was brought up knowing his future lay in the banking world, a career in which he had no interest and probably no talent. Instead, he preferred zoology, although he was also a Tory Member of Parliament. From a young age, he collected insects and butterflies, so it was probably no surprise that he said he wished to have a zoological museum.

In 1908 his parents finally gave in agreed to finance Rothschild's zoological ambitions as well as his international expeditions. At last Walter could throw off the shackles of convention and live as he wished. Well over six feet in height, Walter showed his harmless eccentricities with his animals as he was photographed riding on the back of a giant tortoise – or was it a turtle? On another occasion, he hoped to prove that the African zebra could be a useful animal by taming half a dozen and having them pull a carriage up to Buckingham Palace.

Very shy and with a stutter, Walter did not find a wife to help him in his Buckinghamshire mansion, although one of his two mistresses gave him a daughter. She may or may not have been fond of Walter's bear that was more of a companion than a pet and used to smack the bottoms of visiting ladies. Whether the bear thought of that himself or if the baron taught it is a matter for conjecture.

Rothschild had other animal tricks to irritate his guests, such as accompanying each visitor at a political gathering with a monkey that sat beside him at the table.

Another man with a liking for bears was Shropshire man Mad Jack Mytton. His real name was John, and he was a landowner with a penchant for the dramatic. He lived from 1796 to 1834, so was at his peak during the heyday of Georgian rakehells. He inherited Halston Hall and over 130,000 acres when he was only two years old. His early life included being expelled from Westminster for fighting a master and Harrow for leaving his horse in a tutor's room. He entered Cambridge with two thousand bottles of port to sustain his studies. Finding Cambridge tedious, he embarked on the Grand Tour and then joined the army in time for the occupation of France in the wake of Waterloo. Notorious for gambling and drinking, he left the army having achieved nothing although he remained in the county militia. Mad Jack married twice: his first wife died after two years and his second was sensible enough to run away. Bribing his way into parliament, he was the Tory MP for Shrewsbury and lasted thirty minutes in the Commons before he got fatigued and left.

It was much more interesting owning racehorses and gambling, both of which gave him some success. Possibly because he was bored, he began his career of eccentricity with stunts such as riding a horse up the Grand Staircase of the Bedford Hotel and onto the balcony from where he jumped over the restaurant beneath, horse and all. In common with many English squires, Mad Jack loved hunting, but unlike others, he often hunted naked, even in driving snow. When his horse threw him, and he smashed his ribs, he remounted and continued to ride, uncomplaining.

On one occasion he arrived at a party astride his favourite mount, his pet bear. When he stuck in his spurs, the bear reared and bit his leg. On one occasion, this strange man set his shirt-tail on fire to scare away his hiccups. Wearing only his nightshirt, Mad Jack said 'Damn this hiccup, but I'll frighten it away' and thrust the flame of a candle to his shirt. It caught fire and would have engulfed him if a guest and a servant had not ripped the blazing shirt off him and quenched the flames.

'The hiccup is gone, by God,' Jack said, standing stark naked and unconcerned.

He also liked to pretend he was a highwayman to waylay people he had invited to stay with him. He was a fascinating character but an uncomfortable friend to have, with his two thousand dogs and three thousand shirts, and his constant daring that saw him try to leap a horse and carriage over a toll gate. The carriage smashed to fragments. He allowed his favourite horse Baronet the freedom of the house and the two of them would be seen lying together in front of the fire, while he trained dogs for the fighting ring by going down on his hands and knees and biting them.

On another occasion when he was riding with a friend in a gig he asked if he had ever been in a road accident.

'Why, no,' the man said.

'What a damned slow fellow you must have been all your life,' Mad Jack said and drove the gig up the nearest banking, so it tipped over and toppled both men out.

Despite his vast fortune Mad Jack got into debt and ran to France with a young woman he had met on Westminster Bridge. He made the generous offer of £500 if she came to France with him; she accepted and remained faithful all the rest of his turbulent if short life. Perhaps France also bored him for Mad Jack came back to England and a debtors' prison, where he died. Fittingly, there is a public house named in his honour.

Finally, this chapter will end with a man who was not eccentric in the slightest but who deserves mention purely because he survived in strange circumstances.

As a nation proud of its seagoing history, England has very many stories with maritime associations. There are bloody battles and bold admirals, terrible shipwrecks and famous ships. Sometimes an ordinary seaman also comes to history's attention. Such a man was Thomas Atkins.

In November 1703 a terrific gale hit the southern half of England, wrecking or sinking hundreds of vessels, with eighty sunk off Deal alone. It is hard to imagine the carnage that such a storm could cause to wind-powered vessels with inadequate charts and no lifeboats or other safety equipment. An estimated 1,190 seamen drowned on the notorious Goodwin Sands that terrible month. Diarists recorded the week-long hurricane with John Evelyn saying it was 'not to be paralleled with anything happening in our age or in any history.' He lost two thousand trees in his estate, with an estimated four thousand uprooted in the New Forest and more than seventeen thousand in Kent.

What was bad on land was terrible at sea. The Eddystone Lighthouse was blown down or washed away, taking its designer with it. Eight thousand men died, and hundreds of others crawled onto the Goodwin Sands and hoped for rescue. They were fortunate that the tide was low, for a high tide would cover the Sands and drown them. In Deal, most men and women were too busy salvaging what they could from the scores of wrecks to concern themselves about shipwrecked mariners. One man was more heroic as Thomas Powell set out with a flotilla of boats and rescued two hundred bedraggled survivors.

Given the religious nature of the times, men and women believed that the storm was God showing his anger. Thomas Atkins must have been high in the Almighty's favour. He was a seaman on the fourth-rate HMS *Mary* which went down with the loss of Admiral Beaumont and over two hundred and sixty men. One rogue wave caught Atkins and tossed him from *Mary* onto the deck of nearby *Stirling Castle*. However, *Stirling Castle* was also in difficulties. As she slipped under the sea, another freak wave lifted Atkins and threw him into a small boat which wind and tide pushed ashore to safety. God's finger touched Thomas Atkins that day, and on that strange story, this chapter will close.

Chapter Five
The Female of the Species

In a country, so blessed with eccentric men, it is only natural that the female of the species should also produce a variety of strange and many strong characters. Some of these women have a story that stretches back very far indeed, and such a woman was Black Annis of Leicestershire.

Sometimes she was known as Black Anna, at times as Annie or Agnes and occasionally even as Cat Anna. Black Annis lived in a cave in the Dane Hills, then well to the west of the town of Leicester. Her home was Anna's bower, and there were legends of an underground tunnel that led from the cave to Leicester Castle. There were also legends that she used her viciously sharp nails to claw out the cave from the natural rock. Whatever the stories about Annis, the cave was real; it existed underneath an oak tree.

At one time there was a belief that Annis lay in wait for children clawed them to death, skinned them and hung out their hides like so much washing. That is quite a bundle of evil for one woman, and if anything, the stories prove that she was considered quite a strange and scary character.

It 's hard to say how long Annis' legend had haunted her bower, but she was certainly supposed to be alive and well during the fifteenth-century Wars of the Roses when King Richard III came her way. Annis watched as the king's spurs struck sparks from the stone Bow Bridge. 'It will be his head that hits the stone on his return' she said. The Yorkist king died at the Battle of Bosworth Field, and his body was carried back over the bridge, with his lolling head cracking into the same stone.

Annis's reputation was never good; her name was used as a bogey-woman to scare children while to call somebody a Cat Anna was a deadly insult for the disliked and the shrewish. In the Middle Ages and perhaps before and after, there were either pagan rites or hare hunts around the Dane Hills every Easter Monday, and as a hare was often thought to be a witch, there could be a tenuous connection with Black Annis.

Another sport around the Dane Hills was cat trailing, where horseman dragged a dead cat while a pack of hounds pursued. It is possible that these festivities were originally intended to honour the goddess Eostre, a pagan Germanic deity brought over when the Angles and Saxons first invaded Britain. Apparently, people sometimes saw Eostre as a hare or a rabbit. Now there is a Hare Pie Scramble and bottle kicking contest at nearby Hallaton - another of England's strange sports.

There were stories that people could head Annis's howling from miles away, and the grinding of her teeth made cottagers hide behind locked doors. Herbs were hung above doors and windows to keep Annis at bay, for she was reputed to have very long arms that could reach inside windows and snatch babies and infants. Local lore said that fear of Annis was one reason why Leicester cottages had only one window and that very small.

These obviously grossly exaggerated stories suggest that Annis is not a memory of some mediaeval witch but a folk memory of a much more ancient goddess, a mother spirit of nature that history has demonised into a monster. There were vague stories of child sacrifice here as well, which explained the children's skins hung out to dry. Delving into myths is fascinating, especially when local people have tried to unravel the story.

In the eighteenth-century, a poet and soldier named John Heyrick wrote about Black Annis, claiming she was 'so fierce and wild' with 'vast talons, foul with human flesh' and an 'obscene waist' which 'warm skins of human victims close embraced.' These human skins were the dried hides of the children that Annis had captured, killed and sucked dry of blood. Annis sounds like a lady it would be best to avoid.

There are many stories about this strange creature. One goes something like this:

One Christmas Eve a wicked step-mother sent her three children out to gather firewood. As it grew dark, the children wanted to hurry back for they knew that Black Annis came out at night. They had been safe in daytime for if she emerged then, sunlight would turn her to stone. They heard a strange noise and looked through the witch stone that they carried. Black Annis was emerging from the mouth of her cave and was approaching them through the wood. Naturally, they dropped their bundles of kindling and ran for their skins.

Annis chased them and was catching up but banged her legs on the firewood the children had abandoned and retreated to her cave to put herbs on her cuts. She must have been a fast mover because she caught the children as they arrived home. Fortunately, the children's father appeared at the door with an axe and cracked Annis full in the face. She recoiled, shouting 'Blood!' just as the bells for Christmas began. At their sound, she dissolved into dust.

It is possible that the myths of Annis the ancient goddess have been mixed up with legends of a much later mediaeval witch, the woman who prophesied the death of Richard III. There are many other possibilities for the reality of Annis, but one thing is clear: she was a very strange woman.

Another women, better known, has attracted worldwide interest is also one of the world's first known nudists.

The story of Lady Godiva is famous. The beautiful young woman riding naked through the streets of Coventry with only her long hair covering her modesty and the citizens remaining indoors save for one man, known to history as Peeping Tom, who peered out of his window and in return was struck blind.

This strange tale appears to refer to Lady Godiva, the wife of Leofric, Earl of Mercia and Lord of Coventry. Her contemporaries would know her as *Godgifu*, the Old English form of the name. Godiva was the academic Latin equivalent. Leofric was termed Leofric the Grim, and he ruled over what had once been the independent kingdom of Mercia in the heart of what is now England. This couple did exist. In 1034 Leofric and Godiva founded an abbey on the site of St Osburg's Nunnery, which the Danes had devastated in 1016. According to legend, Lady Godiva ordered all her personal silver and gold melted down and formed into religious items for the new foundation. The remains of this building still stand in Priory Row in Coventry.

Perhaps it was to help pay for this abbey that Leofric of Mercia imposed heavy taxes on the people of Coventry. Godiva, more humane, pleaded with him to ease their burden and Leofric said that he would not do so until she rode naked through the streets. Presumably, he meant it would never happen. Godiva, no stripling teenager but a mature and sensible woman and mother of a son, Aelfgar, surprised her husband by agreeing. Godiva was already a widow when she married Leofric and knew how to handle men. She made preparations for her ride by ordering the citizens to stay inside their houses, to bar the doors and close the shutters so they would not see her naked.

Only when she was sure that the townsfolk had obeyed did Godiva get herself ready. Fortunately, she had long hair, so she shook it loose to cover as much of herself as possible and then stepped onto her faithful steed. Presumably, there was a female groom to help, or somebody had had already prepared her horse.

Did Lady Godiva ride astride or side-saddle? Does it matter? It is more important that she had the daring to do so at all, with the sound of her horse's hooves echoing through the empty streets as nearly all the populace remained obediently indoors. At that time Coventry was not a large settlement, with only sixty-nine families. Godiva may have heard the scrape of wood on wood as a tailor named Tom unbarred his shutters and peered out, only to be instantly struck blind.

Godiva rode on with her long hair shimmering in the sunlight and her horse's hooves raising little puffs of dust from the dirty streets. With her journey complete, Godiva rode up to her husband who presumably was allowed to gaze on the splendour that was his wife. According to legend Leofric kept his end of the bargain and lifted the taxes, retaining only a tax on horses.

There is another version of the story that claims Godiva rode through a crowded Coventry market as the people watched, but a pair of knights ensured that watching was all they did.

There have been suggestions that the whole Lady Godiva story is fabricated, or that it echoes a far earlier tradition of a fertility ritual where local priests took a young girl to a sacred tree at the beginning of spring. Other writers have suggested that Godiva could have been doing penance for some misdeed, in which case she would not be entirely naked but would wear her shift. Another version claims that Leofric had already relieved the taxes and Godiva made her famous ride in an attempt to have the horse tax also reprieved. Peeping Tom may be a much later addition, especially since Thomas is not an Anglo-Saxon name.

Whether or not this ride took place, it is celebrated in Coventry each year by a pageant, and there is no doubt that it makes an entertaining story.

Another woman with associations with nakedness was an Edwardian lady from a manor house in Letcombe Regis, then in Berkshire. She took over the house and true to her period and status was not pleased when she found statues of two naked people in her garden. One was a woman complete with curves and hollows; the other was a man without even a fig leaf to hide the crucial parts. Shielding her eyes, the Lady of the Manor commanded that her servants should throw the offending statues in the lake at once and no peeping!

So in the lake, they were thrown.

About eighty years later the man's statue was recovered. It proved to be a full-size second-century figure of Hercules and fetched some £28,000. The female sculpture was more elusive than the male; despite a search, nobody ever recovered it. However, according to legend, shortly after the Lady ordered her servants to throw both statues into the water, a white female ghost was seen walking along the side of Letcombe Brook, with a story that she had drowned herself after her lover had run off with somebody else. Was that a coincidence?

Although noblewomen tend to be remembered by history, ordinary individuals are usually forgotten. However, taken collectively they could be formidable and best treated with respect. For example, there were the women of Gloucestershire.

In nineteenth-century England, there was a widespread belief that it was legal for a man to beat his wife. Most local newspapers carried tales of such occurrences, with men dragged to court to find out the fallacy of their beliefs and the bruised victim no doubt wondering if she would have to pay further once her nearest and dearest returned to the matrimonial home. Sometimes the situation was reversed, and the wife was the aggressor, but these cases may have been more hidden from the world: no man wished to admit that his wife held the upper hand in his home and castle.

However, there were times that domestic violence became so bad that neighbours stepped in and took matters into their own hands. Such a case occurred in the summer of 1878 in the Forest of Dean.

A miller from Coleford in Gloucestershire was known for his lack of care toward his children and his brutality toward his wife. One thing he also failed to do was send his children to school, which had been obligatory since Forbes' Education Act of 1870. The local magistrates heard about this neglect and summoned the miller to appear at the court to pay the penalty. After an uncomfortable meeting, the miller was angry and frustrated by the time he got home, so his poor wife was once again picked on. As she lay on the ground, bruised and sore, the miller said that his child was next.

The noise alerted his neighbours, and a gang of angry villagers gathered outside the miller's house. The miller, so brave when beating up a lone woman and child, was no hero when the numbers were against him, and forty angry women were thirty-nine more than he was prepared to handle. As he ran up his stairs and tried to hide, the women surged in, grabbed him and dragged him outside, no longer the bully.

Ripping off his trousers, so he was bare from the waist down, they threw him onto his face and whacked his backside raw with whatever sticks and belts they could find. Ignoring his howls and struggles, they then dragged him to his millpond and prepared to duck him in the manner in which men had treated witches, and other women in days gone past. Half naked, humiliated and past car-ing about his image, the bully sank to his bare knees and pleaded for the mercy that he had never shown. Perhaps the women believed that his promises never to strike his wife and child again, or maybe they believed he had suffered enough, but after thoroughly soaking him with buckets of water, they let him go.

Sometimes women merely took on men and beat them at their own game. There are many highway robbers mentioned elsewhere in this book, yet the highway was not the sole preserve of men. Women could also lift a pistol, disguise their face behind a mask, cram on a tricorn hat and mount a horse, riding astride as well as any gallant blade.

Probably the most infamous of these hard-riding women was Moll Cutpurse, whose given name was Mary Frith. Born sometime in the 1580s, she was what was then known as a *rumpscuttle*- a pugnacious, active and somewhat wild tomboy. She was also called a 'very tomrig or hoyden' which is a descriptive phrase that tells what sort of young lady she must have been. Tall and active, in her younger years she learned the skills of wrestling and the quarterstaff, learned to shoot and ride and soon preferred the company of men to women. It soon became apparent that she was trouble, and when the authorities charged her with stealing two shillings, her uncle suggested that she should emigrate to the frontier lands in the New World and even escorted her to the ship. Moll slipped off, swam to shore and headed for London where she became a cutpurse – a pickpocket. Operating around St Paul's Cathedral, Moll's accomplice would act as a decoy to take her victim's attention while Moll did the actual cutting of the purse-strings.

She was successful but also knew the inside of London's prisons, as well as enduring the painful process of being burned on the hand, a quick and simple punishment for thieves. Smoking a pipe or cigar, wearing men's clothes and drinking any man under the table, Moll claimed she was not sexually attracted to anybody, but she moved easily between the world of men and of women. As such, she made an excellent pimp and could find women for men, and suitably respectable men for frustrated or bored married women

From that sordid beginning, Moll moved up the ladder to become a successful fence, receiving stolen goods and selling them off in a shop that was often visited by the victims. Moll soon gained a reputation as a woman it was better to have as a friend than an enemy. Naturally, she was constantly in trouble and once had to stand at St Paul's Cross wearing a white sheet of repentance for 'wearing indecent and manly apparel.' In her own words: 'They might as soon have shamed a Black Dog as Me'. For a bet, she rode from Charing Cross to Shoreditch wearing male clothes and pretended to herself that she was 'Squiresse to Dulcinea of Tobosso'. To show she was not ashamed she blew a trumpet and carried a banner throughout the journey. At Bishopsgate a 'plaguey Orange Wench' recognised her and shouted out:

'Mal Cutpurse on Horseback'

A mob rose, shouting, pointing and yelling: 'Come down thou shame of Women, or we will pull thee down', and Moll had to run for shelter.

For her exploits, she gained the name The Roaring Girl. At that period London was plagued by drunken young gentlemen who erupted from the inns and taverns and amused themselves by bullying innocent passers-by. These rowdy hooligans were known as 'roaring boys' so people placed Moll in a similar category. As a sideline, Moll performed at various theatres. She also married Lewknor Markham in 1614, possibly out of affection, probably a business arrangement to give her the image of respectability during her appearances in court.

At home in Fleet Street, Moll kept a beautiful house, with three maids and parrots as well as the mastiffs she bred and cared for better than most households treated their children.

With the advent of the Civil War, Moll realised that she was a Royalist and although she was in her late fifties, expanded her operations to include highway robbery. Possibly her most famous exploit is her robbery of General Sir Thomas Fairfax. She pointed her pistol at him on Hounslow Heath and ignored his two escorts. There was an exchange of gunfire, Moll shot Fairfax in the arm and killed one of the servant's horses, and off she galloped with 250 gold jacobuses, each worth about a pound sterling. However, it was not a good idea to rob one of Cromwell's generals, and the authorities captured Moll at Turnham Green when her horse went lame. Bribing her way to freedom, she died in 1659 at a decent old age.

Daniel Defoe may have had Moll in mind when he wrote Moll Flanders, which gives her a new twist. One wonders if there were more women like Moll than people realise?

Other women used different methods to gain their ends. Today very few people will know about the Ascott Martyrs of 1873, but in their day they were national celebrities. At that time farm labourers worked incredibly long hours for little pay and the National Agricultural Labourers Union were struggling to have their wages raised to fourteen shillings – that is seventy pence, a week. In Crown Farm at Ascott-under-Wychwood, some labourers only earned eight shillings or forty pence a week. When the men went on strike, the farmer, Robert Hambridge, brought in labourers who were not union men to do the work. Enter the women; forty of whom surrounded the blacklegs and tried to sweet talk them into not breaking the strike.

Robert Hambridge was not having any of this and called the police, who sided with him and arrested some sixteen of the Ascott women. Despite the local magistrates asking Hambridge to drop the charges, he persisted, and the women appeared before the Police Court in Chipping Norton. The judge sentenced seven women to ten days in prison with hard labour and nine to seven days with hard labour. Less than impressed, the local people gathered to voice their protest. An attempt to rescue the women failed so instead there was a mini-riot, with windows and street lamps smashed until around midnight the crowd withdrew.

In the very early hours of the morning, more police arrived from Oxford and loaded the women into four open horse drays for the journey to Oxford jail. When they began their sentence, three thousand people attended a protest meeting and raised £80 to help. There was also a petition sent to the queen and questions asked in parliament. Victoria was not amused to hear that women were so victimised and issued a free pardon and gave each a red flannel petticoat.

Although mainstream history has all-but forgotten them, there is a wooden seat on the village green at Ascott-under-Wychwood, with a placard that states:

This seat was erected to celebrate the centenary of the Ascott Martyrs, the 16 women who were sent to prison in 1873 for the part they played in the founding of the Agricultural Workers Union when they were sent over the hills to glory.

Less sobering but more strange was the marriage custom in Kirton-in-Lindsey in Lincolnshire. In the bad old days, a newly-married husband would take over all his bride's assets and liabilities, including her debts. A Kirton bride-to-be could cancel her debts simply by stripping naked and walking from her house to that of her future husband. Although this practice eased the financial worries of newly-weds, it seems to have died out. One wonders if a similar get-out clause would apply to modern men and if so, how many would take the option?

To close this chapter, a few words about prostitutes, women who are often reviled but who work in what has often been called the oldest profession in the world, as well as one of the most dangerous. England has always had its fair share of such hard-working and hard-used women. At the Stourbridge Fair, which was held every St Bartholomew's Day at Chesterton near Cambridge, so many ladies of pleasure descended that the town-crier was encouraged to use his whip to drive them away.

Such a practise was followed to a much greater degree on Shrove Tuesday, when apprentices in London declared open day on prostitutes and freely attacked them, demolishing brothels into the bargain. The Shrove Tuesday Riot of 1668 was particularly ferocious, partly because it extended well beyond the single day.

The official line was that the attacks were to show the immorality of the court of King Charles II, the Merry Monarch. Back then London had around 20,000 apprentices, roughly one in five of the population, and they were bound to their Master from the age of eleven until they were full grown men of twenty-four. Apprentices were unpaid or at best poorly paid, ill-treated, badly fed and bound to obey strict rules that included no drinking, no violence, no sex and no marriage. Merry England was not so merry for such as them, it seems.

Of course, expected behaviour and the reality are often different, and the apprentices were notorious for violence and drinking, with xenophobia and brawling at football matches added for good measure. So their lives were not always calm, but why attack prostitutes?

There were between 3,500 and 10,000 prostitutes in seventeenth-century London, and they were blamed for a lot of the crime and for leading young men astray from the paths of righteousness. Often the authorities would turn a blind eye if an apprentice thumped one of these obviously-evil women who taunted and teased the poor innocent lad until he became tainted with her vice. One apprentice named Thomas Savage met his end at Tyburn in 1668 and gave a step-by-step confession to show his progress from decent-young-man to a depraved murderer. It was a simple little tale:

The first sin... was Sabbath-breaking, thereby I got acquaintance with bad company, and so went to the alehouse and to the bawdy house: there I was persuaded to rob my master and also murder this poor innocent creature, for which I come to this shameful end.

Elizabeth Cresswell, a high-class prostitute who had two of her brothels destroyed by apprentices in 1668, helped create a petition to none other than Lady Castlemaine, the mistress of the Merry Monarch, and thus obviously the head-harlot in England. The petition, written in the form of a pamphlet was entitled 'The Poor-Whores Petition' and was sent to: 'the most Splendid, Illustrious, Serene and Eminent Lady of Pleasure, the Countess of CASTLEMAINE.'

It started by saying the petitioners were 'countenanced in the practice of our Venerial pleasures -a Trade wherein your Ladyship hath great Experience' and continued by complaining that 'through the Rage and Malice of a Company of London-Apprentices, and other malicious and very bad persons... [we] have sustained the loss of our habitations, Trades and Employments' After that the pamphlet asked for 'some speedy relief... To prevent Out Utter Ruine and Undoing' before these 'evil disposed persons... Come to your Honours Pallace, and bring contempt upon your worshipping of Venus, the great Goddess whom we all adore.'

However, it ends with references to the Pope which gave the game away that it was not a genuine plea but a slanted attack on Catholicism in general and Lady Castlemaine in particular. In essence, it was a savage reminder that the people of England were aware that the court at

Whitehall was a palace of pleasure and sin on a large scale.

Although there was no intercession to help the poor beleaguered prostitutes of London, a judge sentenced eight of the apprentices to death.

Royals and the elite often dallied with illicit sex of course. During the Regency, Queen Caroline was not a model of virtue, and the Duke of Kent kept Madame St Laurent as a mistress for twenty-seven years. When the Duke eventually married somebody else, Madame St Laurent retired to a convent. Compare that to Mrs Jordan's terms to become the mistress of the Duke of Clarence in 1791: '£1200 a year annuity, an equipage, and her children by all parties provided for'. Mrs Jordan was a successful actress who was treated as a royal wife until she fell out of favour, as such women usually did.

Although London prostitutes often had a bad press, sometimes they were licenced by the very church that denied them burial in consecrated ground. That was the case around Redcross in London. The Bishop of Winchester owned the lands, and all the many prostitutes were known as Winchester Geese. In his 1598 Survey of London, John Stow stated:

> These single women were forbidden the rights of the Church, so long as they continued that sinful life, and were excluded from Christian burial, if they were not reconciled before their death. And therefore there was a plot of ground, called the single woman's churchyard, appointed for them, far from the parish church.

The land was known as Cross Bones Graveyard and apparently remains un-consecrated. One wonders if the men who availed themselves of the services of these women spared a single thought for them.

Overall, England had a plethora of interesting women who more than matched their men for style, strangeness, character and often downright roguery. But as well as eccentric men and intriguing women, England has some places that are utterly strange.

Chapter Six
Strange Places

During the early phase of the Napoleonic wars, the French were poised only twenty-two miles away across the English Channel, preparing to invade England and conquer Great Britain. The British press was full of speculation as to what method the French would employ to cross the sea, as with the Royal Navy on patrol, the smaller, weaker and less experienced French navy would have a hard time reaching the English coast.

There were cartoons of the French crossing by balloon or even digging a tunnel under the Channel, but the powers that be in England were more inclined to take the threat seriously than the media were. Prime Minister William Pitt and his fellow Members of Parliament knew exactly how formidable the French army could be – after all it had disposed of every nation in Europe and had already chased the Duke of York's ten thousand men up the hill, down again and back to Britain.

Accordingly, William Pitt ordered a series of small forts known as Martello towers to be built along the coast and told engineers to dig the Royal Military Canal between Rye and Hythe in Kent. The Martello towers were relatively formidable creations armed with powerful artillery, and the canal was England's third line of defence, behind the Navy and the towers. At twenty-eight miles long it formed a boundary between the marshy ground of Romney Marsh and the higher Weald of Kent. At first glance, the idea seems ludicrous. How could a wet ditch a few yards wide stop the French Army that had crossed the Rhine and the Danube and which had defeated every power in Continental Europe?

But no! Pitt had other ideas as well as the military canal. As the British Army was minuscule by continental standards, there were too few men to effectively patrol the banks of the canal yet alone repel an invasion. The Prime Minister had the answer. He ordered that the local authorities placed cardboard models at strategic points to make it appear that the army had a permanent garrison at the canal. That would do the trick!

Although stopping the French was the primary concern, Mr Pitt's Ditch, as the canal was known, was also hoped to prevent smuggling, which was rife in the area.

In reality, Pitt's Ditch was more formidable than it appeared for there were mechanisms in place to empty the contents and thus flood the Romney Marshes, hopefully drowning or at least making life awkward for the invading French. As the French struggled to cross this watery barrier, fresh British reinforcements would march from London. In the meantime, the Royal Navy would pounce on the French ships and landing barges, trapping the invaders in England, ready to be annihilated. Unfortunately, by the time the engineers had dug the canal, the threat of invasion was long gone, so the cardboard soldiers had no opportunity to show their martial skills. Instead, the flesh-and-blood variety were fighting their way through the Iberian Peninsula as well as suffering on various other theatres of war from Canada to the East Indies.

There are other and far older strange places in England. One such is the Cerne Giant just outside the village of Cerne Abbas in Dorset. For those who do not know, the Cerne Giant is a 55 metre, 180 feet, high figure of a naked man carved out of the hillside. He holds a club and boasts impressive masculinity. Other names for him are the Rude Man – for obvious reasons – the Giant, and the Old Man.

This crude fellow is one of many giant hill figures cut into the underlying chalk of southern England. The Cerne Giant is believed to date from the second century AD and is sometimes considered to represent the God Helith. Others believe that it is very much younger and could have been carved out as late as the seventeenth century by the local Lord Holles as a pointed attack on Oliver Cromwell.

Despite these minor academic disagreements, many stories surround the 60-metre-high figure. Local legend says that hunters killed a real giant on the hill and that local people drew around the body and marked him out on the hillside. For obvious reasons, many legends concern the Cerne Giant's fertility powers. One such legend has it that childless couples who made love on a particular part of the figure would soon be blessed with children. There is also the tale that young women who wish to keep their lovers faithful could walk around the hill figure three times. In recent years a fence has been erected around the figure in an attempt to lessen the number of people indulging in these utterly natural and essentially innocent practices. In a world where governments spent billions of pounds on weapons to destroy those with whom they disagree, what could be healthier than a man and woman making love in the hope of creating a baby?

More power to the Cerne Giant!

Not too far away as the crow flies is Silbury Hill, one of the most mysterious sites in England. The largest artificial mound in Europe, Silbury Hill stands proud in Wiltshire and is part of the Avebury World Heritage Site. The builders were active around the same time as the Egyptian pyramids, which must have been a very dynamic period for building throughout the world.

There appears to be nothing inside this hill, no burial of a notable king, queen or holy woman. It is a strange, windy place of great mystery. However, on Palm Sundays, the people of Avebury used to celebrate on the hill with fig trees and sugared water. Why was this place built? To what purpose was it put? We do not know, but it is in an area of intense activity in the Neolithic age. Presumably, it had some ceremonial significance, the purpose of which can only guess. Archaeological digs in the area have found evidence of Roman roads and some mediaeval activity, but it remains a strange, unknown and utterly fascinating site.

Naturally, such a place attracts legends, including one that claimed the Devil was going to dump a pile of dirt on the town of Marlborough, but the Avebury priests outwitted him, and he dropped it on Silbury instead. There is the usual legend of treasure inside, with King Sil clad in golden armour sitting on a golden horse. Others have hazarded that the mound is the Mother Goddess or the Winter Goddess, or an enormous sundial.

But ultimately – we don't know, and that is the truth of the matter.

Other places have less visual impact than Silbury but more ceremony. For instance until the early twentieth century at the ancient stone at Holne in Devon on May morning, a live ram was tied to a granite menhir in Ploy Field; the priests cut its throat and allowed the blood to flow over the stone. Then they roasted the whole animal, including the wool and hide. People scrambled for slices of meat that they considered brought good luck. The day ended with dancing, games and wrestling. Why should one stone bring out such traditions while others have few?

Queen of all the monuments in England is Stonehenge. Enormous and impressive, Stonehenge is a must-see prehistoric monument. Many different theories have been put forward about who built it, when, and why, from the obviously banal to the scientifically possible. Nobody knows the truth, and unless there is some tremendous archaeological breakthrough, it is unlikely that anybody ever will. Some have said that the stones are astronomical calculators. If that is true, and the evidence suggests that it is, then the ancient people were skilled in reading the stars as well as in moving huge objects long distances with minimum technology. But why use stone for such things when there were thousands of much lighter trees to hand? There are theories that such places lie on leylines of natural energy, for which stones act as natural conductors.

However, the stones are considered to have great healing virtues and are a massive draw for visitors, particularly in the summer solstice when druids, pagans and assorted worshippers of the strange, the half-known and the completely made-up gather here to participate in ceremonies that sincerely hope to do only good.

The druids were the priests of the Celts who once owned all the island of Great Britain, including what is now England. The druidic revival, if that is the correct term, put together a patchwork of beliefs, half-forgotten memories and scraps from ancient classical writers, to form some whole that is probably sincerely held and completely benign.

A man named John Aubrey, back in the seventeenth-century when England was obsessed with witchcraft and civil war, put forward the idea that Stonehenge and other stone circles had been temples for the druids. His work was called *Templa Druidum*, and it sparked interest through the succeeding years. By the time that archaeologists discovered that Stonehenge and other stone circles predated the druids and probably the arrival of the Celts into these islands by some hundreds or thousands of years, it was too late. The idea that druidism and sometimes even witchcraft had been performed at Stonehenge was firmly rooted in the popular imagination, and no amount of factual information can shake out strange beliefs.

Who were these druids? As far as we can tell they were slightly more than merely Celtic holy men. Classical scholars such as Pliny, the Elder, writing in the first century AD thought the name equated with 'oak' and 'knowledge', so they had the knowledge of the oak tree, which the Celts apparently held sacred. That brings a memory of Robin Hood's Major Oak in Sherwood Forest to mind and opens the possibility that the mediaeval outlaw was once much more than an archer who pranced around in Lincoln Green. Sacred Oaks and green men loom from the depths of the forest, but that is to digress.

With no contemporary illustrations of the druids, we cannot tell how they looked or dressed, so popular conceptions, strengthened by one mention by Pliny, the Elder, have clad them in long white robes, like monks. Pliny, the Elder also said that druids believed mistletoe to be sacred and used a gold sickle to gather this plant from the oaks where it grew. They were nature worshippers then, at least to a point.

On the 21st June, the summer solstice, druids and others gather at Stonehenge to witness the sun rising above the stones. At dawn, the rising sun aligns the Heel Stone, Slaughter Stone and central Altar Stone, which is a major event in the calendar. As the modern druids gather at the Heel Stone, they encourage the sun's progress by tapping the stone and chanting: 'Arise Oh Sun'. Thankfully, the sun duly obliges.

Stonehenge is only one of England's prehistoric stone circles, of which some have interestingly strange legends attached. The circle at Stanton Dew, south of Bristol is one of these. Many years ago there was a midsummer eve wedding here, with an outdoor feast. It was a Saturday night, and the fiddler was happy to scrape away as the guests danced and pranced and drank and thoroughly enjoyed themselves. As the night progressed, torches were lit to provide light, and the revelry continued. However, when midnight arrived the fiddler stopped playing.

The party-goers protested, begging him to continue. He was adamant that he would not, for it was now early morning on Sunday, and nobody should dance on the Lord's Day. Despite the sometimes quite aggressive complaints, the fiddler stuck to his guns and withdrew to a nearby tree as the bride said that she would have more fiddling, 'even if I have to go to Hell for it.'

As she uttered those words, an old man appeared at the edge of the crowd and said he could act as a fiddler, if the lady still insisted. Naturally, she did, and the dancing continued. This fiddler was devilishly skilled, and the dancers fairly whirled around the grass, skirts flying, feet thumping in time to the music and shrieking and howling with the exhilaration of the music. Some thought the music was a trifle too wild and the celebrations too exuberant but they could not stop however much they wished to.

The dancing lasted until dawn, or literally until the crowing of a farmyard cock. The old fiddler vanished as mysteriously as he had appeared and the dancing stopped. The revellers looked at each other, gasped for breath and immediately turned to stone. Only the original fiddler survived to tell the story of how the stone circle known as the Devil's Wedding gained its name.

There is a similar story attached to the Nine Maidens stone circle on Belstone Common near Okehampton, where a terrible power turned nine young women to stone for dancing on a Sunday. They are said to still dance at noon, although nobody has witnessed that for many years. The stones known as Cornwall's Hurlers on Bodmin Moor were apparently men playing the local game of hurling. Although they were warned not to play on a Sunday, they did and ended up turned to stone. Also in Cornwall is the stone circle known as the Merry Maidens where a group of girls danced for two pipers, a flash of lightning came, and all were petrified, with the pipers sharing their fate a short distance away. The Cornish name is *Dans Maen* which translates as the Dancing stones.

Oxfordshire's Rollright Stones are another strange formation that is worth a visit. Set in some of the loveliest stretches of countryside in England, there are around seventy Rollright Stones, but according to legend, they are impossible to count. The reality of their creation is unknown, so the story will have to do.

Away back in the dawn of time, a small-time king wished to extend his lands to all of England. Taking his bodyguards of knights with him, he climbed the hill beside Long Compton, and quite fortuity met a witch who listened to his hopes and dreams. Her advice was this: 'take seven long strides and look down on the village and you will be the king of all England.'

The king liked that answer and replied with a quick rhyme:

Stick, stock, stone, as King of England I shall be known

The first six strides were fine. On the seventh, a long barrow rose before the king so he could not see the village. Rather than rising to become king of all England, he was turned to stone, as was his following of knights. The witch promptly turned herself into an elder tree for reasons known only to herself.

The king remains in the form of the King's Stone, with his knights forming a circle now termed the King's Men. Nearby are the Whispering Knights.

Unlike the modern druids' gathering at Stonehenge, history records meetings at the Rollright Stones. Every Midsummer Eve people collected here to remember the fate of the king. A man would lop a branch from the witch's elder tree and look for the blood that was said to flow. At that point, the King Stone shifted his head and the Whispering Knights spoke to one another. Those who hoped for a future husband and wife could learn details about them if they listened hard enough. At one time soldiers would chip a sliver off the King Stone to 'be good for England in battle' according to Arthur J Evans in *Folk-Lore* in 1895, while others carried fragments of the stone to bring them luck. That is an interesting story that suggests a very long-standing attachment to the Stones and perhaps a religious significance that extends far deeper than any story of long-gone kings.

Adding to the fun of the area are the fairies who can also be seen dancing around the circle as they emerge from their underground home near the King Stone. Now, what strange story would be complete without a fairy or two?

I will close the chapter with a story from Herefordshire, where a single event links two places: Copse Cross and Old Maid's Walk. Sometime in the seventeenth-century Lord Markey, the landowner of Alton Court near Ross-on-Wye in the south of the county had a daughter named Clara Markey. She was not only stunning but also extremely good natured. She fell in love with her father's gardener, a handsome young man named Roger Mortimer.

However, their relationship was doomed to failure. Although the lovers were close physically, mentally and emotionally, on the social scale, they were on opposite sides of the spectrum. They knew they could never reveal their love, but even so, it came as a terrible shock when Lord Markey told Clara that he had arranged for her to marry one of the sons of the wealthy Rudhall family. There was no way out; at that time daughters had to obey their fathers.

Young Roger Mortimer knew he would no longer see Clara when she was married. He became depressed and walked around in so much of a daze that people thought somebody had bewitched him. At a time when witchcraft was prevalent, the local folk searched for a culprit and instead found a scapegoat in the person of an elderly woman named Nancy Carter.

Old Nancy was dragged out of her cottage and stabbed with pins in an attempt to weaken the supposed spell on Roger, and then straw crosses were placed all around her as a barrier against her presumed evil. There was no mention of the fate of Nancy when Roger jumped into the Wye and drowned himself. Mournful friends carried his body to the Welsh Harp Inn and hired a sin eater.

Sin eaters were people who took on the sins of the recently deceased to ensure they went to heaven and did not remain as a spirit or worse on earth. They were always poor people who could be hired for a small fee such as a loaf of bread and a pint of ale – as long as hirer passed the price over the top of the corpse. In Roger's case, a man named Jack 'the Scrape' Clements took on the job for a quart of beer and sixpence.

'I takes all the consequences, and so I has all the beer.' Clements said happily.

With Roger being a suicide a stake was thrust through his heart before the gravedigger buried him, 'to be sure he would not walk, and bite people in their beds' says the story. Was that an English vampire story in deepest Herefordshire?

The place where the locals buried Roger and other suicides was named Corpse Cross, later modified to Copse Cross, although there are other derivations.

In the meantime, Clara was waiting in emotional agony for her wedding. Taken to Ross Church, the parson gently asked if Clara would accept young Rudhall as her husband. In reply, Clara screamed and fainted. Taken home, she wandered out of the house and onto Roger's grave. Clara did not marry and never quite recovered. Instead, she spent the remainder of her lonely life walking up and down the lane to the grave site, a route that is now known as Old Maid's Walk.

Once again, these are only a sample of the strange places that a wanderer can find throughout England. Some of the smallest and most innocuous have the most interesting stories attached, while others arc simply breath-taking. For the lover of the strange, England is hard to beat.

Chapter Seven
Suffering From an Unhappy Marriage? – Just Sell the Wife

Most marriages have ups and downs, or periods when husband and wife fall out. That is just the nature of the game. Most disagreements are about petty things, such as the type of cat food to buy or the pattern of the wallpaper, or what colour of towels best suit the bathroom. Sometimes things get more serious, and the couple decides that they just cannot live together any longer. Once that decision has been made it is perhaps time for separation, lawyers and the divorce court.

A hundred and sixty years ago, divorce was not an option. Only a private act of parliament followed by the blessing of the church could sanction divorce and although kings and the elite could afford such a thing, the ordinary mass of the population could never afford the £3000 or so it cost. By law and tradition husbands and wives had to stay together until death did them part, and when disagreements and arguments became sufficiently heated for that final solution to become a momentary possibility, they realised they had to do something to solve the situation. A tradition of husbands selling their wives began.

There seems to be no definite start date for this strange idea, yet it was reported in newspapers from at least the 1780s and was current before that date. In the 1690s John Whitehouse of Tipton near Wolverhampton sold his wife to a man named Bracegirdle for an unrecorded sum. Forty years later there was a case in Birmingham when Samuel Whitehouse sold Mary his wife, getting the relatively substantial fee of one guinea for her. Thomas Griffiths, the purchaser, must have been eager to have her especially since part of the agreement was to 'take her with all her faults'. One wonders what these may have been.

Historical documents show over three hundred wife-sales between 1780 and 1850 and possibly there were more that went ahead quietly outwith the probing eyes and scribbling quills of the newspapers. Artists such as Thomas Rowlandson depicted wife sales, and the system seemed to be the same wherever it happened. Although the term 'wife-selling' and the descriptions of the procedure both have indications of a slave market, the reality seems to have been entirely different. The wives, product of an unhappy marriage, were often pleased to be going and hoped for a better partnership with their new man. It seems possible that they already knew who would purchase them, and perhaps there had already been some secret liaison between unhappy wife and prospective buyer to ensure both parties were satisfied with the outcome. There was nothing legal about wife selling, it broke the law and was immoral in just about every way possible. It was also a way out of a nearly impossible situation, and if every party was happy, then the authorities tended not to notice and not to care.

There was one case in 1847 when George Wray of Barrow-upon-Humber had the town crier walk through the town ringing his bell and shouting that Mrs Wray was up for sale at a bargain price.

At first, there were no takers, until a passing seaman tossed over a shilling to take the lady off Wray's hands, with an agreement that Wray should pay back quarter of the purchase price at a later date 'for luck'.

Apparently, the sold wife was pleased with the bargain, took the sailor's arm and the two of them walked off as if much in love.

In another incident in Ninfield in East Sussex, a wife was sold for half a pint of gin, and 'appeared mightily delighted' with the transaction.

On occasion, a man was on quite another mission and just bought a wife on the spur of the moment. Such a thing happened to Henry Brydges, Duke of Chandos when he was at the Pelican Inn at Newbury. He heard a noise in the courtyard and heard that a man was passing by leading his wife to market to sell her. The duke thought the lady was attractive, bought her there and then and later married her himself.

Marriage before 1754 was by consent. The couple announced before witnesses that they were married and that seems to have been that. However, people did not accept such simplicity and wished something more formal to mark both the beginning and termination of a marriage. That led to the practice of wife-selling, so it became nearly normal for the husband to bring his wife to market and sell her there with a rope tied around her waist or neck. One such occasion was recorded in the *Hereford Times* when a man took his wife to a pig market and sold her for a shilling.

> 'Well done, Jack,' somebody shouted. 'that is eleven pence more than I would give; it's too much, boy, too much.'
> 'Well,' said Jack, 'here's the shilling and I warn't I'll make her put the victuals on the table for me... be you willing, missis, to leave him and take me for better or worse?'
> 'I be willing.'
> 'And be you willing to sell her for what I bid, master?'
> 'I be' the man said, 'and will give you the rope into the bargain.'

The rope, with wife attached, was handed over and Jack walked out of the pig market leading his newly bought wife by the halter. Not all sales were so amicable, with the same newspaper reporting cases where the wife was on her knees in tears and begging not to be sold. There was a Hereford butcher who sold his wife for £1 four shillings and a bowl of punch. Sometimes women were sold when wearing only their shift in the belief that this further humiliation would cancel all their debts.

In some cases, men appear to have considered their wives as merely another possession, like a horse or a shiny new hat. Perhaps it was this attitude that made the procedure of wife-selling possible. The system was fixed; the husband officially registered his wife for sale at the local market, tied a rope around her waist, wrist or even neck and mounted her on an auction block as if she was an item of livestock or a sack of potatoes. In theory the woman would be sold to the highest bidder; in fact, the buyer was already usually already agreed, and only the price would be haggled over. The husband may well have advertised the sale in the local paper - that is how such procedures are known – and everybody who was interested would come along to watch the fun. As soon as the new husband bought his future wife, the ex-husband joined the happy pair in the nearest pub. All three celebrated their new conditions in happy unison.

It may sound like a strange system, but it also seems to be reasonably civilised and more amicable than most divorces that unhappy couples settle in court.

In other cases, it is possible that the wife was unwilling and her husband indeed sold her to a total stranger for the highest bid. It is possible to imagine her feelings as she stood on the auction block: humiliation, fear, horror, despair – or perhaps some relief that she was finally getting rid of a husband who one could only describe as a brute at best and a monster at worst.

It has been said, perhaps with some accuracy, that many women demanded their husbands sell them, as a way out of an intolerable marriage, or because they already had privately arranged for a buyer who they liked more. Were the sales a product of a previous affair? It is unlikely that the truth will ever be fully known. The peak period for such things, or perhaps for reporting such things, was in the 1820s and 1830s.

There was one instance in Canterbury in 1820 when a man tried to auction his wife at the cattle market. When the auctioneer refused to have anything to do with the procedure the husband placed the unhappy woman in a cattle pen and asked for bidders. At first, there was none, but after some persuasion, he got five shillings and was quite happy with the bargain.

Sometimes the price was far above the norm, which makes one suspect that the auction was genuine and some more wealthy man took an interest in the lady concerned. Such a case occurred in Chipping Norton in 1855 when an eager, would-be husband paid the enormous sum of £25 for a new wife. However, the local people were not happy with this arrangement and brought into play that other strange old English tradition of rough music.

Hour after hour people gathered outside the new husband's house clattering pots and pans and banging sticks against pieces of wood while making bad poetry about what was happening inside. On the third night an effigy of the purchaser was burned, and on the next day he gave in and handed back his new wife- paying the old husband for the privilege.

Rough music was employed to show the general public's displeasure over the actions of one or more of their neighbours. It came into play in Gainsborough, Lincolnshire in 1836 when a man sold his daughter to a man who promptly emigrated with her to the United States. When the local community found out, they carried his effigy to the seller's house, broke in, wrecked the place and forced him to ride the stang to the accompaniment of raucous music.

Riding the stang was a thoroughly unpleasant experience for the victim. He or she would be hoisted astride a pole and carried bouncing around the parish as the mob hooted, jeered and subjected him to a barrage of missiles. If it was a man was lucky, the crowd would dump him in a local pond. If he were unlucky, his fellow parishioners would beat him up into the bargain. If the miscreant were a female husband-beater, the villagers would parade her around the parish and then throw her into the pond after her uncomfortable trip through the village. Usually, the stang was a simple length of wood, but in Upton Bishop, in Herefordshire, the stang was an ash pole festooned with stinging nettles and decorated with a ram's skull.

After Queen Victoria ascended the throne, the moral tone of the nation altered and many of the old practices faded away. The eventual prison sentence of six months seems very lenient for a practice that, despite its defenders, could at its worst be likened to slavery.

In 1857 the Divorce Act passed through Parliament, and gradually wife selling became a thing of the past. The last one recorded so far was in a police court in Leeds in 1913 when a husband sold his wife to a work mate for a pound, although there are vague rumours of one in Northumberland as late as 1972.

To slightly alter the subject, there were at least a couple of distinguished Englishmen who obtained their wives in dubious circumstances and had long and apparently successful marriages.

Samuel Baker was one of the most likeable of nineteenth-century English explorers. He bought the Transylvanian born Florence, then aged fourteen, at an Ottoman slave market at Vidin and took her with him to explore the River Nile. They later married, and when Queen Victoria knighted Baker, Florence became Lady Baker.

Sir Harry Smith was a young British officer during the Peninsula War. He took part in the siege of Badajoz where a very young Spanish lady sought his protection. Her name was Juana Maria, and the pair were married very shortly afterwards. They remained happily married for many years. The town of Ladysmith in South Africa took its name from her. And on that happy note, this chapter will end.

Chapter Eight
Black Days and Broomsticks

In the seventeenth-century, people were far more scared of witches than people are now of mass murderers. They had more reason for while a murderer could only kill you, a witch could meddle with your immortal soul. Given the fear and the superstition in which people lived, it was not surprising that a man such as Mathew Hopkins should come along, exploit the situation and enjoy mass adulation a hero.

His date of birth is uncertain but was around 1620, and at the age of 24, he began a three-year career that made him both feared and notorious through eastern England in general and East Anglia in particular.

With witch hunts in full cry across the country, Hopkins announced himself as Witchfinder General and set out looking for these terrible witches. He began his hunting in March 1644 together with a man named John Stearne. Tradition claims that the pair of them discovered around three hundred witches and ensured that they ended their nefarious careers hanging from a gallows.

Given the short length of Hopkins' career, his success rate was horrifyingly impressive.

Strangely, for a man so skilled in sniffing out evil, Hopkins had no real experience in witchcraft or in meeting witches before he began his crusade. The son of a vicar, he was born in Great Wenham in Suffolk and had five siblings and rarely seems to have strayed from his part of the world. At some point before 1644, he moved to Manningtree in Essex, and there are rumours that he may have trained as a lawyer at some time. Overall, that was hardly a brilliant apprenticeship for a man who would become a byword for witch-hunting.

It was while Hopkins was at Manningtree that he claimed to have heard women discussing their meetings with the devil and he decided that he would become a witchfinder. That was it: one casual overheard conversation. Hopkins would know that there was no requirement to prove any acts of witchcraft, only make them confess that they had made some association with the devil. Contrary to popular belief, in England condemned witches were not burned at the stake; instead, they faced the slightly more humane penalty of being hanged.

Hopkins and Stearne worked in East Anglia and the counties immediately to the east where Puritan influence was at its greatest. One of their success stories was in Chelmsford where they accused twenty-three women of witchcraft. The court sentenced nineteen of these women to hang; the other four died in prison.

If a woman refused to confess to witchcraft Hopkins and Stearn had various methods of persuasion. There was sleep deprivation which as anybody who has ever had young children knows is as disruptive a form of torture as it is possible to get. There was pricking, whereby three inch long spikes were thrust into the cringing body of the accused to search for the devil's mark, which was the place where the devil had pinched the witch to make her his own. According to witch finding lore, a witch had no feelings in this part and therefore should not feel the thrust of the spike. Of course, after a woman had been subjected to God-alone knows how many great pins jabbed into various parts of her body, she might be in such a state that one more assault was one too many.

Hopkins had women with him who were expert in the art of thrusting prickers into suspected witches. Hopkins also had the nasty little trick of pretending to cut their arms with a blunt knife, and when there was no flow of blood, the woman was obviously a witch.

If all else failed, there was the water test when women were tied thumb-to-toe and thrown into a pool of water. If they floated or 'swam' they were witches; if they did not then, they were innocent, if probably drowned. All in all, things did not look good for any woman or man accused of witchcraft.

Hopkins' career was spectacular as he carved a gouge through eastern England, accusing, torturing and hanging witches, would-be-witches or women that others thought could be, should be or possibly looked like witches. He was paid well for his work, with a special tax levied in some towns to ensure a witch-free environment. In 1647 he wrote the book *The Discovery of Witches* and retired to Manningtree, Essex where he died in August that year. His name is still known.

But why did people such as Hopkins exist? And why did the people of England come to believe in witchcraft?

Well, it was not only England. Fear of witches spread right across Europe at the time, with a less sophisticated public accepting the words of Exodus 22: 18 in the King James Bible 'thou shalt not suffer a witch to live'. As well as commissioning this most famous Bible in the world, King James himself wrote about witchcraft, arguably influenced by his wife. His book *Daemonologie* is only one of a series of witch-orientated volumes that affected the way people thought, of which the most influential was Heinrich Kramer's *Malleus Maleficarum, The Hammer of the Witches*, published in 1487.

The ensuing hysteria proved fatal for a huge number of women and men. Estimates suggest that around 100,000 people were accused of witchcraft in Europe with some 40,000 executed. England, as the example of Hopkins shows, was not immune for this Europe-wide frenzy.

Arguably England's most notorious encounter with witchcraft was the Pendle Witch Trials of 1612. Of the twenty people accused, sixteen were women and, as might be expected in a small community, many were related. Some also had nicknames that reflected their witch-like behaviour. For example, Elizabeth Southerns, also known as Demdike, was accused along with her daughter, Elizabeth Device, and her grandchildren James and Alizon Device. One of the suspects, Margaret Pearson, was tried on three charges including murder by witchcraft, was found not guilty of that but guilty of bewitching a horse, for which she was sentenced to stand in the pillory for four days. That sounds a relatively innocuous sentence when compared to execution, but when one thinks of a woman fastened in a cramped position for hours hideously exposed to taunts, insults and missiles of a hostile crowd, any sense of leniency disappears.

There were two distinct groups of witches at the trials: the Witches of Pendle Forest and the Witches of Samlesbury, although the authorities discharged four of the latter before the trial.

Demdike or Elizabeth Southerns was about eighty years old. If one were to picture the caricature of a witch, Demdike would fit the frame. She claimed fifty years' experience of witchcraft, lived with a cat and was not the prettiest of people. She was one of the witches of Pendle Forest, which was an extensive area of hilly woodland in Lancashire, North-western England. It had once a royal hunting preserve and by the seventeenth century had already been encroached upon by agriculture. During Demdike's trial, her accusers said she brought up her children and grandchildren as witches and apparently 'no man near them was free from danger.'

Anne Whittle or Chattox was another elderly lady, nearly blind and no friend of Demdike's. They seem to have been rivals in witchcraft and supposedly caused cattle disease, crop failure, flood, storm, famine and human sickness in their section of Lancashire. The coven of Pendle Forest Witches met at a location known as Malkin Tower on Good Friday, 10th April 1612. Possibly because it is one of the few recorded, this meeting is arguably the most infamous in England. There are no remains of Malkin Tower, and nobody knows exactly where it was, what it looked like or even if it was a tower at all. However, local wisdom suggests it was near the Cross Gaits Inn- trust the English to have a pub nearby.

It was on 21st March 1612 that Demdike's grand-daughter Alizon met a Halifax pedlar named John Law. She asked to buy some pins, but he turned her down, possibly because he suspected she had some demoniac use for them. When Law collapsed and died soon after, suspicion fell on Alizon, who was arrested along with her grandmother and two other suspected witches. The authorities shoved them in cells within Lancaster Castle.

The remainder of the Pendle Forest coven met at the tower to discuss an escape plan. It is strange that rather than plan something that used their supposed supernatural powers, they intended the very prosaic method of blowing up Lancaster Castle. They also wished to murder Mr McCovell, the governor. According to legend once the witches left the tower they jumped onto their familiars, which were horses, and galloped away. Eight of the people who attended the meeting were arrested and accused of witchcraft.

Before the authorities took Ann Whittle to trial, they accused her of 'wicked and devilish arts' and of murdering Robert Nutter by witchcraft. During her examination, Chattox explained that about fifteen years previously she had sold her soul to the devil and had a Familiar called Fancy. Chattox also admitted that Nutter had insulted her daughter, Anne Redferne and she had put a 'bad wish' on him. Further to that, she had placed a spell on a man named John Device when he stopped paying her blackmail of a sack of meal annually. He had also died. There were other, lesser charges that she admitted and, to her credit, asked the court to be lenient to her daughter. To the court's discredit, they were not.

Elizabeth Southerns or Demdike also made a confession in which she says that she met the spirit of the devil 'in the shape of a boy' who offered her anything she wished for in exchange for her soul. The spirit's name was Tibb and Demdike agreed. Tibb appeared around 'daylight gate' from time to time, asking what Southerns wished from him, but she usually said 'nay, nothing'.

Tibb could appear as a black cat, and on one occasion the spirit appeared as a brown dog at a time Demdike had a baby on her knee. When Tibb began to suck blood from her left arm, Demdike screamed out: 'Jesus save my child!' At the name of Jesus, the dog vanished, and Demdike said she was deranged for the next couple of months. Demdike also mentioned an incident when she asked a miller named Richard Baldwin for payment due to her daughter. Instead, Baldwin threw them both off his property, calling them 'whores and witches' and saying he would see one hanged and the other burned. After that, Demdike was more receptive to Tibb and agreed the spirit should help them gain revenge on Baldwin.

Demdike or Southerns gave no details of her revenge. Instead, she advised murder-by-witchcraft. Apparently, the trick is to 'make a picture of clay, like unto the shape of the person they mean to kill' and 'take a thorn or pill, and prick it in that part of the image you would have to be ill.' Burning the picture would end the person's life, although there would be chanting and spells to help the murder. Demdike, old and infirm, died in prison, which was not surprising given the terrible conditions in such places. She saved herself the ordeal of the trial and inevitable subsequent execution.

The trial was notable for two things. The first was the ability of a magistrate named Roger Nowell to elicit a detailed confession from various witches. The second was the evidence given by one particular witness, the nine-year-old Jennet Device, which led to the hanging of ten people including her own family. Jennet was one of Demdike's grandchildren and the sister of Alizon and James. During the trial, Jennet gave measured evidence against her own family as the accused implicated each other and heaped blame on blame.

Jennet was so small that she had to stand on a table to give evidence, but her words ring through the years:

My mother is a witch and that I know to be true. I have seen her spirit in the likeness of a brown dog, which she called Ball. The dog did ask what she would have him do and she answered that she would have him help her to kill.

Among the six people that Jennet named were her mother and brother. When Jennet's brother James also pointed the fatal finger at his mother, Jennet added to the woes by saying he had also been a witch for the past three years. As if murder, attempted murder and terrorism were not enough, the witches were also accused of creating butter from skimmed milk and making beer turn sour. Demdike's daughter, Alizon's mother, had the horrendous experience of being stripped and thoroughly searched until an extra nipple was found, for the use of Satan of course.

There was no waiting for appeals or reprieves. The day after the trial finished, the authorities hanged all those convicted of being witches. Ironically, twenty years later, Jennet was also accused of witchcraft, and it was a child who named her. She was found guilty, but this time the authorities demanded more evidence. Her accused later admitted that he made everything up.

When the ripples of interest over the Pendle trial still washing across England, there was another, scarcely less sensational eruption of witchcraft in Belvoir Castle, the home of the Earl and Countess of Rutland. The witches in question had all been servants in the castle: Joan Flower and her two daughters Philippa and Margaret. They did not disguise the fact that they were witches, which was probably unwise given the tension of the times, and people even viewed their cat Rutterkin with suspicion. Joan was described as being untidy with deep-set eyes and had a reputation as a herbalist.

When Philippa was caught stealing, the Countess was probably glad to be rid of the whole bunch of Flowers and very lenient to only sack them rather than opting for a more dramatic punishment.

However, the Flowers did not view things in the same light and called on three other known witches to hatch a plot of revenge against their erstwhile employers. One of these witches was Ellen Green, who had a variety of familiars including a mole, which was unusual, and a kitten, which was not. Another was Anne Baker who had visions, and the third was Joan Willimott, who had gone over to the 'other' side when her mother had blown an evil spirit into her mouth. Others say that it was not her mother who did this but her Satanic master and the spirit was in the form of a fairy named Pretty.

These charming women caused all sorts of problems for the Earl and Countess including killing their offspring, with one son, Henry, Lord Ross, being bewitched by the simple expedient of stealing his glove, thrusting pins through it and boiling it. As an encore the Flowers cursed the Earl and Countess as well, ensuring they could have no more children.

In 1617 or 1618 the Flowers and their friends were arrested, taken to Lincoln jail and charged with witchcraft. According to legend Joan Flower refused to confess, despite whatever torments her interrogators used. Eventually, she asked for bread and butter, which her jailors kindly provided, saying that she would choke if she were guilty of witchcraft. Strangely, she choked and died, or so the legend claims.

After the death of their mother, the Flower sisters both confessed. They agreed that Rutterkin the cat was their mother's familiar and that spirits had sucked at them in the past. They were both hanged.

There is a strange postscript to this tale. Bottesford Church in Leicestershire has a monument that depicts the Earl, and Countess Rutland kneeling with their dead children and the words 'bewitch'd to death.' However much we disbelieve in witchcraft in our enlightened age, in the past it was a real fear that blighted many lives; the Earl and his Lady sincerely believed that the Flowers had murdered their son by witchcraft.

There were many witch stories the length and breadth of England, and one of the most persistent and widespread was the belief that witches could transform into hares. These animals are usually the calmest in the animal kingdom but display some sexual schizophrenia in early spring when Mad March Hare syndrome takes over, and they indulge in frenzied boxing matches in fields and meadows. Perhaps it is this sudden switch of personalities that encouraged people to equate them with witches. A recorded spell allowed the witches to transform themselves:

> I shall go into a hare, with sorrow and such and mickle care
> And I shall go in the Devil's name, aye, while I come home again.

There was a belief that hares could alter their sex and many stories of them being shot and wounded, with local women or men later discovered with gunshot wounds. Apparently, it took a silver bullet to kill a witch, though, so perhaps ordinary lead only wounded.

Hares and folklore were historically intertwined. Boudicca herself was supposed to have set a hare before her as she squared up her Iceni army before the Roman invaders. The idea was not to scare the enemy with witchcraft but to have her druids read the future in its erratic running. Hares are involved in all sorts of strange folk belief. For example, pregnant women were well advised to avoid the animal unless they wish the child they are carrying to have a hare-lip, while a hare's foot a sure way of preventing rheumatism and flatulence. Eating hare's flesh was a sure-fire beauty aid, but with an unfortunate side effect of causing depression. All sound witchy stuff.

Witchcraft ceased to be a legal offence in 1736, but a government order cannot remove belief in such things.

People abused suspected witches for very much longer, and there was even an official trial in the 1940s. Witches issued curses for the same length of time so whatever one's personal belief it is perhaps better to walk warily of things one does not completely understand.

Chapter Nine
The Hellfire Club

It could only start in England. The very name gives an idea to the type of society that many novelists have used to their advantage. The Hellfire Club was a society, or a network of societies for the wildest rakes of the *ton*, where the members expected excess and discarded respectability. But what was the Hellfire Club and how did it gain its notorious reputation?

For a start, there was not just one Hellfire Club, but a number spread over England and Ireland, and not all were called Hellfire at the time. Probably the most infamous of these gatherings was Sir Francis Dashwood's Order of the Friars of St Francis of Wycombe. What a splendid name to camouflage the reality of their exploits. The men were high class, often political and undoubtedly secretive with an inner society, The Order of the Second Circle hidden within the first. Dashwood's group met from around 1749 to perhaps 1766. Nobody knows for certain, although in the 1760s Brooke's Club in London was closely associated. It is Dashwood's society that most often features in romantic novels, with Sir Francis portrayed as a typical eighteenth-century rakehell, out for wild adventure, drink and women. Yet he was not the earliest of the Hellfires.

In 1718 Philip Duke of Wharton founded the first of these clubs. Wharton was an oxymoronic character, part intellectual, part drunken wastrel. His companions seem to have been of similar ilk and stature, as far as anybody can ascertain, with the Earl of Hillsborough, the Earl of Lichfield and Sir Edward O'Brien suspected of being members. The members called themselves devils, scoffed at religion and named the president of the club as the devil himself. Even more shockingly, the club admitted women on equal terms with men – an aspiration to which some present-day golf clubs could emulate. Strangely, although women could indulge in all the activities, they were not allowed into one of the meeting places, the Greyhound Tavern.

What did the members of this infamous club do? Well, that is open to conjecture. Some say they were merely a talking and debating society with mock religious ceremonies and some sort of role-play with members pretending to be characters from the Bible.

Other such drinking and blasphemy clubs followed, which brings us back to Dashwood. His club initially met at the George and Vulture pub from 1746. With a motto of *Fais ce que tu voudras*, which translates as *Do what thou will*, the club sounded as if it was open to any excess but in reality, the tales that survive seem to be more of serious practical jokes mingled with heavy drinking and sex than of evil devil worship.

Membership was initially limited to twelve and Dash-wood was the prime mover. On one occasion he pretended to be the King of Sweden while at the Court of the Csar at St Petersburg in Russia. At the time the two were mortal enemies so it would have been easy for Dashwood to create a diplomatic incident or even provoke a war. It would be good to know more, including what Benjamin Franklin was doing in the society. Unfortunately, all the records were destroyed, which is maddeningly frustrating when one wishes to find scandal, intrigue and strange goings-on. However, despite its reputation, Dashwood's club was apparently never known as a Hellfire Club at the time.

In 1751 Dashwood moved his club's operations to Medmenham Abbey, which is where most of the wildest tales were born. He carved out caves beneath the abbey and had them decorated with various sexual images. The members were said to have sacrificed to Bacchus, the drinking god, and Venus the goddess of love. The members called each other brother and brought in what they called nuns – presumably prostitutes – to add to the fun. It seems to have been little more than an upper-class swingers club with drinking, bawdy humour and sex. The legends of black magic and devilish practices came much later after the club was long dead and buried.

So what was the reality?

The few surviving documents give clues that this was nothing more serious than a drinking club: eighteenth century. In 1779 a book, *Nocturnal Revels* gave some details and stated that at meetings:

For the improvement of mirth, pleasantry, and gaiety, every member is allowed to introduce a Lady of cheerful lively disposition, to improve the general hilarity. Male visitors are also permitted, under certain restrictions, their greatest recommendation being their merit wit and humour.

Heavy drinking was encouraged, and there was music but – strangely -

No indelicacy or indecency is allowed to be intruded without a severe penalty; and a jeu de mots must not border too much upon a loose double entendre to be received with applause.

However, the female guests were to consider *themselves as the lawful wives of the bretheren during their stay within the monastic walls; every Monk being religiously scrupulous not to infringe upon the nuptial alliance of any other brother.*

In the 1760s the members of Dashwood's club included some of the cream of society. There was Sir Francis Dashwood, Lord le Despencer, the poet, Paul Whitehead and the Earl of Sandwich, First Lord of the Admiralty. There was a clutch of politicians: Lord Melcombe Regis and Sir William Stanhope, MP, Sir John Dashwood-King, MP, John Tucker MP, and John Wilkes MP. There was Thomas Potter, son of the Archbishop of Canterbury and Dr Thomas Thompson, Physician to the Prince of Wales, Sir Henry Vansittart, Governor of Bengal and MP for Reading and Robert Vansittart, Regius Professor of Civil Law at Oxford. The list reads like a Who's Who of the supposedly great and the good, the soured cream of the nation.

Were these men bound to devil worship? Hardly: it may have been a wild place by the standards of the time, but history and novels had added a sinister reputation to what sounds more like a club for immature men who had never left behind the ploys of their schooldays. It is only strange that such a harmless, if raucous and foolish, collection of clubs could gain such a bad press.

Chapter Ten
Strange Creatures, Dragons

Every country has its stories of strange beasts, from Bigfoot in North America to the Yeti of the Himalayas and the Loch Ness Monster in Scotland, but only dragon legends seem to be universal. Were there ever beasts called dragons that roamed the countryside terrorising villages and fighting knights? It seems unlikely that these flying, fire-breathing creatures ever existed, but the persistence of legends across Europe including England tends to make one wonder. Is there any truth behind the many stories?

Although England's patron saint is Saint George, who won everlasting fame for fighting and killing a dragon, to some, the white dragon is a representation of England itself, as the red dragon is to Wales.

There is a Welsh legend that talks of a long-standing battle between a red and a white dragon, where the red dragon is the indigenous British and the white dragon the invading Anglo-Saxons. The red dragon's cry was so powerful that on hearing it men became powerless and women lost their children. To cure this horror the British people worked out where the exhausted dragons would fall after fighting, so they dug a deep pit to hold the creatures when they fell. They landed in Oxford, reputedly the very centre of the island of Britain and once caught; the dragons were drugged with mead and buried in Snowdonia, North Wales.

The dragons' later tale is mixed up with Merlin, whose life, true or false, does not belong here; he was arguably more likely to hail from Wales or southern Scotland than England.

Dragon banners were common in old England. For instance, in 752 the West Saxons or Wessex men had a golden dragon as a banner at the Battle of Burford, while the Bayeux Tapestry has two dragons associated with the Saxon King Harold. Sir Walter Scott was well aware of the association between the Saxons and dragons. In his poem, *The Saxon War Song* he begins:

Whet the bright steel, Sons of the White Dragon!
Kindle the torch, Daughter of Hengist

Trust Sir Walter to catch the essence in a single line!

Later English kings also sported dragon banners, with Henry III, Edward I, Edward III at Crecy and Henry V at Agincourt, all marching under a dragon, while the Yorkist side during the Wars of the Roses also sported a dragon. These creatures may be mythical, but their images were relevant to thousands of men who fought in their shadow.

The Wessex dragon still flies every Midsummer Eve in Burford, Oxfordshire where the local school has a dragon ceremony to celebrate the eighth-century victory of Wessex over Mercia. For lovers of strange English traditions, there are Morris dancers as well. Burford, of course, is an attractive town that also has the ghost of Sir Lawrence Tanfield and Lady Tanfield who ride their coach and four across the rooftops. Burford folk saw the Tanfields frequently until some bright person trapped them in a bottle and dropped them into the river. Until the nineteenth century, the local people ensured they remained under the surface by pouring in water whenever the river level dropped in dry summers. But that is to digress from dragon-lore to that of the supernatural.

Even in this enlightened twenty-first century, Dragons have not disappeared from the mainstream of English life. As late as 2003 Archbishop Rowan Williams appeared at his enthronement at Canterbury with two dragons woven on his silk robes; one was red, the other white.

With all this imagery, it is not surprising to hear that there are stories of actual dragons running rampant around England. The best-known may be the Lambton Worm from County Durham. When John Lambton was supposed to be in the church, he went fishing in the River Wear instead, despite the warnings of an old man that no good would come of it. Lambton hooked a young dragon he thought was an eel and threw it down a well. It seemed to thrive down there, grew large and escaped.

The villagers saw its terrible trail as it coiled around a hill; they shivered in horror as the dragon ate children and livestock and for years they lived in terror behind locked doors and barred windows. John Lambton came back after seven years away, perhaps on a crusade, and learned about the horror his actions had unleashed. Unsure what to do, he asked a local wise-woman how he should destroy the creature. She gave him a protective suit of armour covered in arrowheads, told him to kill the dragon and then said he had also to kill the first living thing he met once he had done so.

Thus prepared, Lambton faced the dragon down. Always ready to kill and destroy, it coiled around him, but the arrowheads on Lambton's armour cut it to pieces. Lambton lifted the shredded remains of the dragon and threw them in the river. The fight had been short and bloody, and the knight had won.

However, although Lambton had succeeded in disposing of the dragon, the next living thing he met was his father. He remembered the wise woman's words and knew he had to kill his own blood. Lambton refused to do so. Rather than commit patricide, he killed his pet dog. That did not answer, and for the next nine generations, the Lambtons lived under a curse.

A county to the north of Durham, Northumberland has its very own dragon at Longwitton. There are few details except that it lived near three wells, it had a long tail, warty skin that dripped poison, sharp claws and a black tongue. Apparently, the wells had magic properties and healed any wounds that a would-be dragon slayer made in the beast. However, a knight named Sir Guy of Warwick disposed of this warty pest by riding between the dragon and the wells and thrusting his sword down its throat.

There was also the forest dragon of St Leonards that appeared as late as 1614. The local description was a 'strange and monstrous serpent lately discovered and yet living to the great Annoyance and divers Slaughters of both Men and Cattell'. It was nine feet long shaped like the axle-tree of a cart, had large feet and 'shot forth venom'. There seems no record of the 'divers' 'men and catell' it slaughtered because rival local lore hinted that it lived mainly on rabbits.

Even later was the dragon that landed in an Essex field in 1669. Complete with wings, it did no damage and soon left again. This brief visit inspired commercial activity selling model dragons at the local fair. Most English dragon tales are of this nature, ephemeral, vague as a politician's promise and backed with mythology rather than hard facts.

With England being different to every other country in the world, it is natural that English dragons should also be distinct. The English version is known as a wyvern, and there are similarities as well as differences. The wyvern has the same sort of head as a dragon, with the body of a giant lizard and a pair of wings, but has two legs rather than four. Of course, the wyvern breathed fire and could attack and demolish villages if it chose but it could not speak, which is a skill that foreign dragons have. Like most people in England, it is a poor linguist. There are said to be neither dragons nor wyverns left now, with the English knights having followed the example of Saint George and hunted them to extinction.

Sometimes the demise of the wyverns could be sad. In Mordiford in Herefordshire, a little girl named Maud found a wyvern when it was just a baby, 'no bigger than a cucumber' and brought it up. She fed it saucers of milk as if it was a pet kitten and kept it safe in the forest. The two, wyvern and little girl grew very attached to each other, to the consternation of Maud's parents.

However, dragons need nourishment other than milk, and as Maud's wyvern grew, it began to hunt for more substantial food. Mice, poultry and rabbits fell victim, and then sheep and cattle until inevitably the wyvern started to eat humans as well. It lived in Haugh Wood, with a well-beaten path known as Serpent Lane that led from its lair to the confluence of the Rivers Wye and Lugg. Only Maud was safe from the Herefordshire wyvern as it steadily reduced the population. Luckily for Herefordshire, a passing knight named Garston killed the wyvern with his lance and the community breathed again. It was unfortunate that Maud arrived just as Garston delivered the death-blow. The knight left as Maud wept by the side of her friend.

There were alternative endings that featured a condemned man who was granted his life if he killed the beast. Various stories say the man caught the dragon sleeping and chopped it to bits, hid inside an empty cider barrel and shot it through the bung-hole or rolled a barrel studded with spikes onto the creature. All these versions agree that the dragon-slayer died soon after because the wyvern had poisonous breath.

Dragon legends are harder to kill than dragons seemed to be. As late as 1875 two women carried a pair of newts into the church at Mordiford and tried to drown them in the font to ensure they did not grow into dragons.

There is another dragon legend from that same dragon-haunted village. Apparently King Arthur's nephew Mordred was marching to fight some enemy and forded the River Wye, which allegedly is why this spot is Mordred's Ford or Mordiford. He won his battle, grabbed the enemy's green dragon banner and handed it to the nearest church. For centuries after, a dragon was painted on the west wall of Mordiford Church.

Some dragon legends are elusive, but there are tales of dragons seen fighting on the banks of the River Stour on the border between Suffolk and Essex in September 1449. One dragon was black, the other apparently 'reddish and spotted' with the fight lasting an hour before the black dragon withdrew. The place was named Sharpfight Meadow.

Of course, St George's victim is probably the best-known dragon in English history. The original story is not English but seems to come from Georgia in the eleventh century, so presumably, the Crusaders brought it to England. The story says that a dragon was terrorising a village called Lasia, so the locals fed it two sheep a day in an attempt to appease it. The creature demanded more, so the villagers fed it children instead, with each child selected by lot. Eventually, the king's daughter was chosen. Grief-stricken, the king offered half of all his treasure if the villagers chose somebody else. The people were having none of it; they had seen their children sacrificed so why should they spare a princess? As was the custom, the princess dressed as a bride and marched bravely to be slaughtered. Fortunately, St George happened along, made the sign of the cross and captured the dragon.

He led it back to Silene and said he would kill it if the people converted to Christianity, which the king and fifteen thousand of his subjects did.

The story may represent Christianity's victory over the dragon of paganism, or good over evil, with the dragon as the devil, but it also shows some disturbing class consciousness with one level of society – the princess – represented as more valuable than ordinary villagers. Anyway, England adopted St George as the patron saint and never looked back. As Shakespeare said:

'Cry God for Harry, England and Saint George!'

Chapter Eleven
More Strange Creatures

Dragons are only one of the strange creatures that have infested the English countryside. There have been all types of dogs and hounds and mysterious creatures, but few vampires.

Vampires are thought to belong to Transylvania or the screen, but London had its own version in a cemetery in Highgate. The story does not belong to the days of gothic romance or even high Victorians but as recently as the 1960s and 1970s when the sound of the Beatles was blasting over Britain and youth culture was spreading from Liverpool around the world. It was a group of these young people who entered the cemetery to test out their theories on the occult. At that time Highgate Cemetery in North London was not looking its best, tangled with weeds and with gravestones gloomy and neglected looming through the murk.

It was December 1969 when David Farrant who later ran the British Psychic and Occult society, decided that he would camp overnight among the gravestones. He survived the experience, despite seeing some grey creature slipping through the dark. It was a couple of months before he reported the incident to the local newspaper, and almost immediately other people also admitted that they had seen strange things in the cemetery. There was no single entity, but a variety, from a phantom on a bicycle, a man walking in a pond and a tall man wearing a hat. There was even a man calling himself Sam Manchester who claimed that what he termed a King Vampire of the Undead had been buried here in the eighteenth- century. This unearthly man had been carried from what is now Romania in a coffin and existed in London's West End before being buried where Highgate Cemetery later spread. The actions of the youths or others who dabbled in the black arts had wakened the Romanian vampire who now haunted the cemetery, looking for victims.

Except for a scattered handful, the vampire sightings faded away as the 1970s died, but in 2016 more than one person saw a strange thing, a man wearing Victorian clothing and a top hat, floating through locked gates. Is there a vampire in Highgate Cemetery? Or did the undoubtedly creepy atmosphere delude people into believing they had seen something?

Apart from vampires, there have been various animals roaming the otherwise -pretty-placid English countryside, such as the Surrey Puma in the 1960s, the Fen Tiger and the Peak Panther, but these were thought to be flesh-and-blood creatures escaped from a zoo or private collection.

The Beast of Bodmin is different. It is nearly as well known in England as the Loch Ness Monster is in Scotland. Rather than a Highland loch, the Beast infests the lonely Bodmin Moor in Cornwall and appears from time to time. It is not a monster as such, but people have described it as a phantom wild cat the size of a panther that attacks and kills animals including cattle. There are doubters of course, who say that creatures such as a panther could not survive in the English climate and that there is simply not sufficient food on a Cornish moor. Others say that the sightings are of wildcats that have escaped from zoos or merely feral cats. However in 1995, a boy found the skull of a large cat by the River Fowey, and sightings continue.

In the 1980s Devon was alarmed by various sightings of a creature with 'bulging green eyes' that slaughtered sheep and provided the local Royal Marines with a live exercise in tracking. Although some of the best snipers in the world hunted with night-sights and enthusiasm, they could not kill the creature whose screams echoed through the dark. Eventually one of the world's crack military formations decided that enough was enough and left the beast alone. Saying that the green-eyed-monster was merely a wild dog, they beat a tactical and strategic retreat. That round went to the Beast of Bodmin.

England has other strange creatures that infest the lonely byways. For example, there is the gytrash. Few people today report seeing such a thing, but in the past, any journey in the north of England could be rendered perilous by the presence of a gytrash. These shape-shifting creatures would approach the traveller in the guise of a friendly dog with a wagging tail and lolling tongue, or perhaps a strayed donkey or pony. The traveller would be deceived, and the gytrash would lead him or her away into a dark and lonely place before either vanishing or transforming into its true self.

The fear of the gytrash is mentioned in *Jane Eyre* when Jane wonders if Mr Rochester's dog Pilot could be such a beast. Early accounts describe the Gytrash as a huge black dog with glowing red eyes, but it could be any variety of dog or pony. Perhaps the onset of the motor car has scared the Gytrash away, or maybe they are still around, waiting for the lonely traveller.

A creature that was suspiciously similar to the gytrash was the Black Shuck. This creature was also a black dog that unwary travellers could come across as they traversed the countryside. In some accounts the Black Shuck was specific to the sixteenth century, in others, it frequented many parts of England at various time periods, but was usually around seven feet long and manifested only when thunder and lightning tormented the land. In either case, the Shuck's paws burned the ground wherever it stood, but it was its eyes that mattered for if they met the gaze of a traveller that person was immediately struck dead with a heart attack. Shuck preferred to wait at crossroads or churchyards for its victim and could be heard baying to the moon. Some have seen him at Stowmarket in Suffolk with the head of a dog and the body of a black-robed monk as it guards the Clopton hall treasure.

St Felix has the blame for burying this treasure for reasons that are unclear. He gave his treasure two guards, a monk and a white dog, which combination has created the folk story of the half-monk, half- hound-guardian. There is also a dog named Padfoot that is in the area, which may be another name for Shuck.

In August 1577 Black Shuck struck terror across Sussex. First, he knocked a steeple through the roof of a church in Blythburgh, killing three of the congregation. Then Shuck left through the door, gouging great scrapes in the wood. Next, he appeared at Bungay and disposed of another trio before a storm whizzed him away. So what was this Shuck? Was it some supernatural creature bent on destruction? Or was it only the natural power of the wind?

Even worse than the Shuck were the Hellhounds of Dartmoor away down the deep south west of the country. In such a green and pleasant land as England, it could come as a shock to find oneself in the desolation of Dartmoor. It seems a perfect location for a Gothic horror story and the Hellhounds, or Yeth hounds kindly oblige.

According to legend, these Yeth hounds are the crazed souls of unborn children, cursed to roam the moors until doomsday. Like the Shuck, these were great black dogs with evil eyes, but unlike the Shuck, they hunted in a pack. They came out at night, with their eyes gleaming red as they scoured the mist-tormented wastes for human prey. To hear their terrible hunting cry is to be driven crazy by fear and to be caught is infinitely worse as they capture their prey and drag it into some awful netherworld of hell. Dartmoor is an excellent place for such creatures. The landscape is as wild as anywhere in Southern England, with gaunt stone tors protruding from bleak moorland, frequent rain and winds that sweep in from the huge expanse of the Atlantic, yet there is also a surreal beauty that nobody can deny.

Sometimes the Yeth hounds are known as Wisht Hounds or the Wild Hunt of Devon. The idea of a pack of wild supernatural creatures careening across the countryside hunting something or somebody is not confined to England, yet it seems to be prevalent in Devon. Is that because Devon clung to its Celtic ancestry and traditions while other parts of the country adopted the Germanic culture of the Anglo-Saxons?

Nobody seems exactly sure what this hunt is, or perhaps if anybody witnesses this wild spectral mob chasing them, the sight scares away all desire to investigate further. The only thing that most legends have in common is that a sighting of the Wild Hunt is a portent of disaster, a harbinger of doom.

The Wild Hunt of Devon seems to be a combination of spirits and hounds. As always many variations may indicate layers of folklore added at different times or merely alternative versions of the same story. The hunters may be fairies or the dead returning to their old haunts. Others have even included legendary historical figures with the Hunt as well as sundry Norse gods. The Norse gods may indicate an Anglo-Saxon influence, as they shared many of the same deities, albeit with slightly different names.

One strange myth that must be relatively recent claims that Francis Drake, who was a maritime adventurer and pirate, leaves Buckland Abbey to join the hunt. Drake has quite a character in the strange department; he was one of Elizabethan England's finest seamen, albeit of loose morals where piracy was concerned. There are also stories that he sold his soul to the devil in exchange for maritime prowess and as well as his human crew he was captain of a legion of demons. As the Spanish called him *El Draque*, the Dragon, they would undoubtedly have agreed.

One legend that attached itself to Drake concerned his behaviour when the Spanish Armada was sighted approaching the Channel. The sanitised version claims that he finished his game of bowls before he set to sea. The other version says that he borrowed a length of wood and a hatchet and chopped off chunks of wood. Drake's demonic powers changed the wood-chips into ships that fell into the sea, caught fire and scattered the Spaniards' initial invasion attempt. To make sure of victory, Drake then called up a coven of witches who met at Devil's Point and whistled for the wind. The resulting storms battered the Spanish right around the coasts of the British Isles. This episode occurred not long before the great witch scares of the late sixteenth and early seventeenth centuries.

Drake's other enduring legend concerns his drum. Ever since he died, the story spread that whenever England needed his help, a drum would summon him from whatever region of the afterlife he inhabits. Drake's drum also rolls its message when the country is at war. That may sound like supernatural nonsense, but at the end of the First World War when the Imperial German fleet was about to surrender, the sound of Drake's drum echoed through the flagship of the Royal Navy. A search of the ship found nothing. Was Drake signalling in triumph? Or was he warning the Navy that the Germans intended to scuttle their fleet in Scapa Floe?

All very interesting perhaps, but a long way from the Wild Hunt. Drake is said to leave Buckland Abbey in a black carriage hauled by a team of headless horses. However, pray that you don't see him for, in this case, Sir Francis is a portent of death. One last comment about

Drake: when Nelson began his series of victories against the French, some thought that he was a reincarnation of Drake. The Devon connection was strong.

Another local in the Hunt carries the strange name Old Crockern and has associations with Wistman's Wood. Old Crockern seems to be a spirit of the moors, grey in colour, with deep-set eyes. Perhaps he is a folk memory of some pagan god or spirit? There is a tor named Crockern Tor, but which came first, the legend or the name, the spirit or the stories? Was this tor once worshipped as a god? Or did the god inhabit the tor? Now Old Crockern is one of the Riders, a single figure from a dimly remembered religion hunting the unknown across the vastness of desolation.

Legends claim that Old Crockern stables his hellhounds at Wistman's Woods, where the Hunt is said to begin so he may be of more importance than a mere rider. He may be the Master of the Hounds. Yet the Wood is small, if very atmospheric. They are also undoubtedly old, with wind-tortured trees and a plethora of cracked granite underfoot that is dangerous to unwary ankles but hardly the home of hounds of Hell. Perhaps they were larger once, or something happened here to begin the legend.

Herefordshire and Shropshire also have a version of the Wild Hunt that rides the storm clouds. In the Shropshire version, a Saxon landowner named Edric fought back against the Normans in the aftermath of Hastings. Two Welsh kings, Rhiwallon and Bleddyn, joined in Edric's private war. Together they held the Normans at bay for four years in which the Saxon earned the name of Wild Edric. It is said to be Edric who leads the local Wild Hunt that appears when black times threaten.

If you are lucky enough to be in the Burnley area of Lancashire, then wander up to Eagle's Crag on Cliviger Gorge and observe. Lord William Towneley leads the local Wild Hunt, and the show should be worth watching. According to myth, he will once again attempt to seduce the witch named Sybil while she was in her other form of a doe. That would be worth watching.

Perhaps even stranger is the black slug of Bleaklow Hill in north Derbyshire. This creature infests the Long-denvale Valley and people who claim to have seen it mention its rolling eyes. Occasionally a phantom lorry is seen in the same place; hardly a strange beast but a sign of changing times perhaps. Overall, England has a unique selection of strange beasts.

Chapter Twelve
The Strange Woman
in Wych Elm

Some things are so mysterious that even the most bizarre speculations appear an attempt at rationalisation. Such a case is the unfortunate woman whose skeleton was found buried inside a tree. She has been named Bella, although nobody knows anything definite about her. However, there are rumours and speculation.

The known story started in April 1943, a time when the world was in turmoil and forces of evil were undoubtedly afoot. Hitler's War was three-and-a-half years old, Britain's armies were heavily engaged around the Mediterranean, and in Burma, convoys were facing the torpedoes of the U-boats to bring food and munitions to Britain, and the home fires were burning fiercely.

When all that was happening, back in Stourbridge in the West Midlands four young boys were in Hagley Woods searching for bird's eggs. They were climbing an ancient wych elm when fifteen-year-old Bob Farmer came across the skull of a woman thrust into the hollow trunk. A quick examination showed that the skull had crooked teeth and was fairly recent as there was still some hair clinging to the flesh on the forehead.

After initial hesitation, the boys sensibly informed the police, who found a nearly entire female skeleton inside the tree. They found more: one of the woman's hands had been chopped off and buried nearby while there were pieces of clothing minus the labels, a pair of worn shoes and a gold ring. A crumpled length of taffeta had also been thrust into the mouth of the skull, suggesting the woman had been suffocated to death and then crammed into the hollow trunk.

Police enquiries found out that local people had heard somebody screaming about a year and a half previously. The pathologist, James Webster worked out that the woman had indeed died around eighteen months ago. She had been a mother about five feet tall, and although she had visited a dentist, the police could not find any files that matched her. Not yet baffled, the police trawled through the records of around three thousand missing persons – to no avail. That was as far as the police got; the case of the mysterious skeleton faded away as the war continued to grind on.

It was over a year later, the winter of 1943 that interest in the case was re-ignited when a spate of graffiti appeared on local buildings, with questions such as: 'Who put Luebella down the wych-elm? Or 'Who put Bella in the wych-elm?'

A theory began that a coven of witches or some practitioner of black magic had stuffed the woman – now thought of as Bella – into the tree. That story was bounced around for a while and then died away until 1953 when a letter to the Wolverhampton *Express and Star* put forward another idea. Somebody calling themselves Anna of Claverly suggested that Bella had been involved in a German spy ring during the war.

Anna said that Bella's real name was Una Mossop and her husband Jack had worked at one of the many local munitions factories. As with so many at that time, the Mossops had needed money, but then Jack had providentially met a Dutchman who offered money in exchange for information about local factories. The Dutchman had been a German spy and had passed on the information to the next in the link, a man who worked in a theatre. On one occasion Jack had met the Dutchman at a pub beside Hagley Wood. A Dutch woman had been present and had argued with Jack's contact.

The Dutchman ordered Jack to drive them out to Hagley Wood at the Clent Hills where the Dutchman strangled the woman. Jack was shocked but a man in his position – a traitor to his country - had no choice but to stay silent. Both men hid the body inside the elm tree. According to this version of the story, Jack later had a nervous breakdown, was committed to a lunatic asylum in 1941 and died the same year.

Was that possible? The year would make sense, but would a factory worker in 1940 or 1941 be able to afford a car or have the petrol to run it at a time of severe rationing? Would he be so willing to turn traitor? Would Jack's information be sufficiently useful to be worth buying? Were there honestly so many German agents running loose around the Heart of England?

The answers will probably never be known. Personally, I prefer the coven of witches story, but there again, I am strange by name and nature.

Chapter Thirteen
Strangely Romantic Criminals

England has a strange fascination with criminals. There are numerous accounts of Jack the Ripper, the Great Train Robbers and even the Kray Twins, while earlier ages were obsessed with highwaymen, smugglers and Robin Hood the outlaw. A gloss of romance has been painted over these men, making them appear daring and glamorous rather than the desperate fugitives they must have been.

As Robin Hood is the earliest of these villains, I will feature him first. There are as many legends about Robin Hood as there are books and films made about him. The favourite image is of a dashing, handsome man dressed in Lincoln green, with a band of laughing archers behind him and the beautiful Maid Marion at hand. This band of happy outlaws lived in Sherwood Forest and never failed to outwit the dastardly Sheriff of Nottingham and the evil King John. All good, rousing stuff, if completely untrue.

It was 1377, about a hundred and sixty years after King John's time that the first known written reference to the bold Robin came into existence. There are manuscripts in the British Museum that claim Robin was born in a place called Lockersley around 1160. Another source claims he was from Wakefield and was active around 1322, so you pays your money and takes your choice.

One thing these supposed facts have in common was the general idea that Robin Hood came from Northern England. There are stories all over the North in which he features, from an archery contest in Whitby to his exploits around Nottingham. Equally nearly certain was his delight in robbing the rich to give to the poor.

However, much of our modern perception of Robin Hood comes from the nineteenth-century pen of Walter Scott. He used the title Robin of Locksley and gave the story elements of a struggle between Norman knights and Saxon yeomen. It was also Scott who elevated Robin's skill at archery to make him a marksman capable of splitting one arrow with another. In reality, English armies only became renowned for archery in the late thirteenth century. The first major English victory in which archers were predominant was Edward I's victory of Falkirk in 1298 – and the archers were Welsh rather than English. So Scott created both the Saxon-Norman theme and Robin's enhanced skill with the bow.

There is little variety in accounts of the death of Robin Hood. Perhaps it was the nature of the life he led, but as he aged, Robin became sick. Accompanied by Little John, he journeyed to Kirklees Priory near Huddersfield where his aunt was the Prioress – allowing Robin the respectability of rank. He hoped that his aunt would be able to help him; instead, a knight named Sir Roger de

Doncaster encouraged her to kill him. No family loyalty among the Hoods, then.

Pretending friendship, the gentle Prioress bled Robin so be was progressively weaker. Knowing he was dying, Robin blew his horn to summon the faithful Little John. Unfortunately, John was too late to help. Asking John to give him his bow, Robin fired an arrow and John buried him where it landed. His burial mound is still visible in Kirklees Park.

Maid Marion does not feature in any of the early accounts of Robin Hood. Robin's lover seems to be a later invention from May plays of perhaps the fifteenth or sixteenth century.

Although the legend and the name of Robin Hood have come down through the centuries, albeit highly embellished, they show mainly the heroic, positive side of chivalry and righteousness. Time has removed the grim reality of the period with the harsh lives of the peasants or the reason that so many men and women had to live outside the law. It is perhaps also typical of the strange English idea of romanticising criminality and making these bad men as colourful characters. In an age of repressive government, outlaws such as Robin Hood were the only way the downtrodden could strike back against their oppressors; Robin was the personification of resistance. It is possibly more ironic than strange that it was a Scottish Conservative who added the final touches to the character and time-period of a man who has become not merely an English, but also an international folk hero.

A few hundred years later highwaymen also garnered a fund of romantic stories around them, as if somehow there was something poetic about being held up by a masked man with a pistol on some lonely stretch of road, terrified out of one's wits and robbed of all one had.

Some names of these mounted thieves have come down to us through time. There is Dick Turpin of course, with his famous ride to York, William Davis the Golden Farmer, Plunkett and Maclaine whose fictional exploits were made into a film and Jack Rann, known as Sixteen String Jack.

One of the earliest recorded Highwaymen was John Popham. He read law at Balliol College, Oxford but preferred drinking and whoring with his dissolute companions. He slid into a career of highway robbery until his wife convinced him that lawyers were made more money without the risk of being caught and hanged. Lawyers also had the bonus that they spent their nights caressing a warm wife rather than clutching a cold pistol at the side of the road.

In time Popham became Lord Chief Justice during the reign of King James VI and I. In this capacity, he spoke to a highwayman on trial for his life. Popham asked if any of his former colleagues were still active and the man replied, 'All are hanged, my lord, except you and me.'

Other early highwaymen included Gamaliel Ratsey, charmingly known as Gamaliel Hobgoblin because of the incredibly ugly mask he wore. He adopted the image of Robin Hood as he gave some of his takings to the poor. It is doubtful if he only targeted the wealthy, however.

Another kind of highwayman was Isaac Atkinson. He came from a well-to-do family and spent his youth in amorous adventures. He managed to infuriate his neighbours, particularly those fathers whose daughters he seduced and abandoned and the husbands whose wives had preferred young Atkinson's favours to the marital bed. In an age before ready contraception, it was inevitable that a number of mini-Atkinsons should begin to populate the countryside, so either through his father's disfavour or a desire to escape his obligations, young Isaac Atkinson grabbed a horse, mask and gun and took to the freedom of thieving on the open road.

Atkinson seemed to favour robbing attorneys as he hunted the highways and byways of Norfolk, making a good living until he altered his target to include young women. One, in particular, took his attention, especially since she was well shaped and carried a bag of gold. As Atkinson approached, the woman tossed her bag over a hedge. Torn between the pursuit of sex and the acquisition of wealth, Atkinson chose the latter and dismounted to get the gold. In the meantime, his stallion preferred the sexual option and headed straight for the woman's sleek mare, which bolted with her rider on top and Atkinson's horse cantering lustfully behind.

By the time Atkinson retrieved the treasure his horse had long gone but, he thought, at least it was worth it. Gasping in anticipation, he opened the bag, found it was full of half-pennies rather than gold and began to walk home, dejected, footsore and heart-sick. However, that was his last robbery for the fair woman informed the authorities and Atkinson was hunted down and hanged... And all because of an amorous horse.

Other highwaymen were even less romantic, such as Jacob Halsey, who added rape to robbery when he took a fancy to one good looking victim. 'My pretty lamb,' he said, 'an insurrection of an unruly member obliges me to make use of you on an extraordinary occasion; therefore I must mount thy alluring body, to the end I may come into thee.' Pretty enough words to hide an action as brazen and brutal as any.

Dick Turpin is undoubtedly the best remembered English highwayman, although he was nothing like the stories. Epping Forest in Essex is one area with Turpin legends as he and Tom King were reputed to use this place as a base for their raids. Strangely, a pub in the area prefers to recall Sixteen String Jack, another masked robber who also infested the area.

There is little truth in the Turpin legends and no romance at all. Even his famous twenty-four-hour ride from London to York on Black Bess was false. John 'Swift Nick' Levison performed that particular feat in 1676 after he robbed a seaman in Kent and needed an alibi. Turpin was an Essex man, born sometime in 1705 at the Blue Bell Inn in Hampstead which his father operated. He was said to be 'loose and disorderly' as a youth. He began life as a butcher, rustling animals to fill his shelves until the authorities caught him. He moved from cattle theft to smuggling but the free-traders wanted none of him, and the customs men soon had his measure.

Robbery seemed the best alternative to an honest job, so he joined the Gregory Gang, a group about a dozen strong that was also known as the Essex Gang. These romantic rogues operated against lonely farmhouses, breaking in at the dead of night and torturing terrified women until they surrendered all their possessions. One case at Loughton saw Turpin and his merry band sitting an elderly woman on top of a fire to loosen her tongue. With a reward of £50 announced, it was open season on the Essex Gang, and Turpin fled once more.

Finally, he took to highway robbery, with a short-lived partnership with a man named Thomas Rowden before Turpin struck out on his own. On one occasion he attempted to hold up a fellow highwayman who shouted out:

'What is this: dog eat dog?'

The highwayman proved to be 'Captain' Tom King, who was much more of the loveable if thievish rogue than Turpin ever became. The two teamed up, created a base at Loughton Camp, an Iron Age fort and used a cave in Epping Forest as a look-out spot to spy on potential victims. They robbed everybody from beggars to the wealthy, so no notion of robbing the rich to feed the poor. Turpin became so notorious that in 1737 the reward on his head increased to £100 – which was an astounding amount of money for the eighteenth-century.

Such a figure attracted bounty hunters, and that same year a gamekeeper named Thomas Morris either used his tracking skills to Turpin's lair or came across him by accident. Turpin was at Fairmead Bottom, today ironically near the Robin Hood Roundabout. Either way, the result was the same. Turpin was quicker with his pistol and shot Morris dead. It was the fourth of May 1735, and Turpin had added murder to theft, robbery, assault and torture. The romantic hero had shown his true colours.

From then on Turpin's career took a different direction. Stealing a horse from a man called Major, he named it Black Bess, rode it to London and stabled it at the Red Lion in Whitechapel. In the meantime, Major had taken the loss personally and made enquiries throughout London, described his favourite horse and gave Turpin's name.

Either too canny to come in person or just lucky, Turpin sent Tom King to collect the horse from the Red Lion. The local constables were waiting and promptly arrested King. The next few minutes are confused. It seems that Turpin had been hiding nearby and tried to rescue King, who burst free and rode toward him. Turpin and the constables exchanged fire, with possibly King joining in if he had retained his pistol. In the melee, Turpin managed to shoot King and promptly fled. He may have believed King was dead or he could have been trying to save himself. The truth will never be known.

As he lay dying, King told the constables about the lairs in Epping Forest. Was he trying to save his soul? Or getting some revenge on Turpin, or was he delirious with pain?

In the event, Turpin did not return to Epping Forest. Instead, he moved north and started a new career as John Palmer, horse dealer. With no knowledge of such things, Turpin resorted to stealing horses and selling them on, sometimes even to their previous owners. Living in the Green Dragon Inn at Welton, Yorkshire, Turpin made his final mistake.

It was 1739, and he was possibly drunk when he shot his landlord's gamecock. When a witness objected to this senseless act, Turpin, as John Palmer, threatened to shoot him as well. The authorities promptly thrust him into the local lock-up. Enquiries began, and the magistrates uncovered his recent history of horse stealing. Quickly placed in the more secure cells of York's Debtor's Prison, Turpin wrote to a relative, requesting an alibi. The relative, Turpin's brother-in-law, refused to pay postage on the letter, which was returned to the postmaster. It was an unhappy coincidence that the postmaster had also been Turpin's teacher, and he recognised Turpin's writing. Being an upright citizen, he galloped up the road to York, identified Palmer as Turpin and accepted the now £200 reward, knowing that he was condemning his former pupil to the noose.

At the next assizes, Turpin was found guilty of horse-rustling and sentenced to death on the 22nd March 1739. It was now that Turpin's legend began as he had a whole stream of visitors all wishing to meet the celebrated highwayman. For once Turpin acted the part. He bought spanking new clothes and shiny new shoes, hired a handful of mourners and faced the gallows with courage.

Dragged to his death in the back of an open cart, Turpin showed his best, bowing to the massed crowds. He climbed the ladder to the gibbet without any show of fear, spoke casually to his guards, addressed the audience and recognised the hangman as Thomas Hadfield, once a member of the Gregory Gang. The *York Courant* of 7th April 1739 describes his death:

> *With undaunted courage looked about him, and after speaking a few words to the topsman, he threw himself off the ladder and expired in about five minutes.*

The night after gravediggers buried him, bodysnatchers unearthed Turpin's corpse to sell to anatomists, but somebody stole it back and re-interred it under a layer of quicklime. With his burial, the legend grew.

There have been novels, films and even a television series about the romantic highwayman. Strangely, the legend concealed most of the truth. Today, Hampstead Heath which once enjoyed the reputation of a virtual home from home for Highwaymen has a clump of oaks known as Turpin's Ring as well as the Rose and Crown pub (once the Blue Bell Inn) where a copy of Turpin's birth certificate is displayed. The Spaniard's Inn in the same area also has Turpin memories, for his ghost remains here, and the lucky can sometimes hear the clopping of Black Bess's hooves. More tangible are the leg-irons he wore while he waited to get hanged.

While highwaymen have achieved a good press, even Rudyard Kipling fell under the spell of the smugglers.

> *If you wake at midnight, and hear a horse's feet,*
> *Don't go drawing back the blind, or looking in the street,*
> *Them that ask no questions isn't told a lie.*
> *Watch the wall my darling while the Gentlemen go by.*

Smugglers are also prone to be tagged with the label of romance. Modern day people often consider them as mischievous daredevils, happy-go-lucky rapscallions who dared authority to bring brandy to the parson and silk to the ladies. Some may well have been of that ilk, but others were as vicious criminals as the country has ever seen, prepared to torture and murder to protect their profits and, in reality, often traitors that robbed the nation of badly needed revenue in times of war.

There were some female smugglers of course. One such was Bessie Catchpole who operated on the coasts of Essex and Norfolk. Originally she had been a smuggler's wife, but when the Excisemen killed her husband in a frantic skirmish, Bessie stepped into his sea-boots and took control of his yawl, *Sally*. No shrinking violet, Bessie often dressed as a man, complete with cutlass and reeking pipe. In those years after Waterloo, the country was in a state of depression and the crew welcomed her as captain. When one foolish man laughed at the thought of a woman in charge, Bessie promptly knocked him overboard. That ended any disputes.

According to legend, Bessie did not go a-smuggling on the Sabbath. Nor did she resort to brute force to defeat the revenue but instead used wiles and tricks. On one occasion she was crossing from Dunkirk and ran straight into a small flotilla of Royal Navy ships and revenue cutters. Where other smugglers may have tried to bluster or to turn and run, Bessie steered *Sally* straight for the nearest cutter. However, as she closed, the revenue men saw that she had the yellow fever flag flying from her mizzen. Fearing small-pox, plague or some other horror that would ravage their crowded vessel, the revenue men hoisted all sail and fled. Brave as lions when facing Frenchmen or smugglers, even the stoutest of sailors quailed before disease.

On another occasion Bessie knew that the Excisemen were searching for her so waited for night and doused *Sally*'s lights. She also sunk her casks of smuggled brandy and attached them to the sea-bed with grappling hooks. When morning came, Bessie welcomed the revenue men on board her yawl, allowed them to search where they willed and smiled when they refused her offer of breakfast.

Other smugglers were not as friendly as Bessie. Probably among the worst was the Hawkhurst Gang who operated in Southern England in the 1730s and 1740s. Their headquarters were at Hawkhurst in Kent, and their operations spread as far west as Dorset. As so often in England, an inn featured prominently, as they based themselves in the Oak and Ivy in Hawkhurst. They also frequented the Mermaid in Rye where legend has them drinking with pistols on the table in case of trouble.

If even half of the stories are correct, the ground underneath the Oak and Ivy was perforated with tunnels that led in just about every direction. It seems to have been possible to journey from the Oak and Ivy to the Royal Oak, to the village centre, to the Four Throws or Tubs Lake without even once emerging above ground. The smugglers must have been miners in their spare time.

When not feverishly hacking out tunnels, the Hawkhurst Gang were busy smuggling, although there are more stories about their brutality than about their success in bringing illicit goods into the country. Perhaps this gang used fear as a weapon to keep their operations secret, or maybe they were just an extremely unpleasant crew.

There is one story that says that a body of the gang was revelling at the Mermaid at Rye and left for the Red Lion. High-spirited or just drunk, they walked through the street firing pistols in the air until one young man named James Marshall began asking questions. Some of the smugglers dragged him away, and that was the last ever seen of him.

A gang of this type invariably attracted the worst kind of men. One such was Jeremiah Curtis, alias Pollard, a known smuggler from Hastings. He came with a reputation for violence which he enhanced when he helped murder a farm labourer named Richard Hawkins. Hawkins was from the parish of Yapton in Sussex, and the smugglers suspected him, wrongly as it turned out, of stealing some tea they had hidden on his farm. In January 1748 he was working in his barn when Curtis and a labourer named John Mills burst in and ordered him to go with them. When Hawkins protested the smugglers said if he did not come they would put a bullet through his head.

The smugglers took Hawkins to the back room of a pub named the Dog and Partridge on the common in Slindon. More smugglers including Thomas Winter of Poling and Little Fat Bob, servant to Curtis, were waiting there for them which must have been ominous for poor Hawkins. The smugglers held him prisoner there from mid-afternoon until midnight, all the time interrogating him about the tea he was supposed to have stolen. Either because they did not believe his denials, or out of pure cruelty, they bundled Hawkins onto a horse, whipping and beating him with the handles of their whips until he died.

It was nine months before somebody found Hawkins body, weighed down with stones in a pond in Parham Park in Sussex, then owned by Sir Cecil Bishop. The smugglers later found the tea they thought he had stolen.

Even the Revenue men were often scared to challenge the Hawkhurst Gang, and when they did, the results could be fatal. There was one incident in 1740 outside the village of Hurst Green in East Sussex when a riding officer by the name of Thomas Carswell and a small patrol of dragoons, came across fifteen hundredweight of tea in a barn. Loading the tea into a cart, they were trundling slowly toward Hastings and had reached Silver Hill on the road between Hurst Green and Robertsbridge when thirty smugglers attacked them. Carswell was shot dead and his tiny military escort captured. Official retribution was sure and George Chapman, one of the gang, was caught, tried, hanged and gibbeted on the triangular village green in his home village of Hurst Green.

Four years later the gang was probably at the peak of its powers when three smuggling luggers moored off Pevensey in East Sussex, a noted smuggling centre. The Hawkhurst gang required five hundred pack horses to carry the smuggled goods inland. Such an operation would have required excellent organisational skills as well as a large number of men, so the gang were more than mere brutes; there were brains and expertise behind the savagery.

To counter the actions of such people, the Excisemen used a network of informers, some of whom were motivated by dislike of the smugglers, others who preferred the feel of a coin of the realm between their fingers than the knowledge that their neighbours were enriching themselves illegally. When the Hawkhurst gang captured one of these informers, they dragged him to the lake in their home village and spread-eagled him on the little island so he could only breathe if he held his head up. If the informer relaxed, his mouth would be underwater, and he would drown. He survived a very uncomfortable night and sensibly fled the area.

In 1748 the Hawkhursts hit a major setback. The War of the Austrian Succession was in full swing, the Navy was battling the French across half the oceans of the world, and the Channel was busy with smugglers evading taxes that should be used to pay the Royal Naval seamen. In September 1748 the Customs cutter *Swift* under Captain William Johnston scored a notable success in pursuing and catching a smuggling lugger named *Three Brothers*. The authorities were jubilant as they packed the cargo in the king's warehouse – the Custom House - in Poole. They locked up the thirty-nine casks of brandy, two tons of tea plus quantities of rum and coffee, shoved the lugger's crew in jail and retired to celebrate. With the cargo worth some £500 – many tens of thousands in today's currency – they had reason to be happy.

Either their security was lax, or the smugglers were cleverer than expected for some of the crew slipped out of jail and alerted the Hawkhurst Gang. An alternative story says that the smugglers' crew escaped by small boat and alerted the gang. Either way, the Hawkhurst smugglers plus a gathering of local ne'er-do-wells numbering around thirty men in total broke into the King's Warehouse and emptied it of the tea. Unable to carry the rest, they rode away proud of their night's work.

Not surprisingly, the authorities put up a huge reward of £500 for details leading to the capture of the thieves.

The gang's reputation was about to climax in an incident that both made their notoriety and saw them fated for destruction. With the authorities on the alert for any sight of the gang, they had to be very careful. What follows is only one of many variations of what happened.

Sometime in the 1740s, a Hawkhurst gang member named Diamond was seized in Chichester and slammed into jail. His fate was uncertain, so one of his colleagues named Daniel Chater, a shoemaker from Fordingbridge came forward with an alibi to prove he was innocent of all charges. It was Chater's bad luck that he met a grey-haired revenue man named William Galley in the White Hart Inn, Rowlands Castle. The White Hart was a known smugglers' haunt so both Chater and Galley should have known better. As it happened, it was the landlady, Elizabeth Payne who recognised the revenue man and informed two of her regulars, the smugglers William Jackson and William Carter. The smugglers immediately believed that Chater had turned informant.

Now the Hawkhurst gang plummeted to the depths. Pretending friendship, they plied Galley and Chater with drink until they fell into a drunken stupor on one of the beds. The smugglers had a meeting to decide what next to do. The gentle wives of Jackson and Carter had no doubts: 'Hang the dogs' they said. Instead, the Hawkhurts resolved to keep both men prisoner and then treat them as the courts decided to treat Diamond.

Jackson woke Chater and Galley by running his spurs across their foreheads then slashed them with his horse-whip until they tumbled, bemused and bleeding out of bed. That was only the beginning of their ordeal. As a smuggler named Richards said he would shoot anybody in the inn who mentioned what had happened, Galley and Chater were tied onto a single horse and whipped as they rode along to the Red Lion Inn at Rake.

'Whip 'em,' Jackson shouted, 'Cut 'em, slash 'em, damn 'em' and the entire band of smugglers including Edmund Richards, Little Samuel Downer, William Steele and Harry Sherman joined in. At Harris's Well, they took Galley off his horse, discussed killing him there and then, but continued on their way until Galley fell off. They threw him face down over the saddle with Little Sam torturing him agonisingly as they rode over the Downs.

Believing that Galley was dead, the smugglers hastily dug a pit threw him in. He was still alive but suffocated inside his grave. Some days later a man by the name of Stone found the grave when his hounds sniffed suspiciously at the newly dug ground.

Wishing to make an example of Chater, they chained him up in a filthy turf hut for a few days, debating shooting him and decided that was too simple a death for a man they believed was an informant. Hacking, stabbing and torturing Chater with a clasp knife, they tried to hang him over a thirty-foot well, failed and threw the still living man down to the bottom. As he groaned at the bottom, they pelted him with rocks until they were sure he was dead.

Although smugglers were either tolerated or admired, no community liked to befriend sadistic murderers. In 1747 the gang's leader, Arthur Gray was captured, and next year he was hanged for murdering Thomas Carswell. Although Thomas Kingsmill became the leader, the gang's prestige had peaked, and the descent had started. Driven by fear or distaste, the men of Goudhurst came together into an organisation known as the Goudhurst Band of Militia with an ex-corporal named George Sturt in charge. Promoting himself to become General, he breathed defiance at the smugglers. Led by Thomas Kingsmill, the Hawkhurst gang attacked the village on the 21st April 1747. In a scene that could have come from the Wild West, both sides exchanged fire around the church.

General Sturt proved a capable commander and drove off the smugglers, killing three including Kingsmill's brother. The government turned the screw on a gang that was now in decline, with a reward offered for each smuggler captured and a free pardon for any who turned King's Evidence. It was a similar system as had been used against pirates and proved how seriously the government viewed the menace of smuggling.

One by one the gang members were captured. William Fairall, known as Shepherd; Richard Perin, known as Pain, Thomas Lillywhite, Richard Glover and even Thomas Kingsmill himself were caught and accused of breaking into the Custom House at Poole. Jeremiah Curtis, possibly the most brutal of the entire bunch, escaped, slipped over the sea and joined the Irish Brigade in the army of France. Lillywhite was found not guilty. Glover was guilty but not hanged while Perrin, Fairall and Kingsmill were condemned to death. The hangman 'turned them off' at Tyburn. Kingsmill's dead body was displayed at Godhurts and Fairall's at Horsendown Green.

Jackson, Carter and the others who murdered Galley and Chater were tried at Chichester and condemned to death. Jackson died in prison shortly after being measured for the gibbet; Carter was gibbetted near Rake in Sussex, a man named Tapner at Rook's Hill near Chichester and others at various places. Their rotting corpses remained as examples of justice in what was an incredibly violent age.

The demise of the Hawkhurst Gang did not even dent smuggling as there were many other free-trading gangs up and down the country. Some were merely groups of men who ran the occasional cargo to alleviate poverty while others were professional criminals who added strange names to their tax-dodging criminality. For example, there was The Blues or the South Kent Gang who operated out of Aldington. A rogue with the unusual name of Cephus Quested led them. The name sounds like something out of Harry Potter, or possibly Charles Dickens, but it was authentic. When the authorities hanged Quested in 1821 George Ransley became the leader; a kind judge eventually sent him to Van Diemen's Land, where he died of disease.

There was also the Bowra clan who kept a tight grip on the Groombridge gang of the 1740s. The Mayfield Gang was led by a man with the nickname of Kit Jams, although his given name was Gabriel Thompkins. From time to time they operated alongside the Hawkhurst gang.

Joss Snelling of Broadstairs in Kent used the alias of John Sharp and led the Callis Court gang of the late eighteenth century. It was a bit of a family affair with his son and grandson eventually involved. Snelling used a small vessel called *Bee* and escaped many encounters with the revenue. However, he was involved in one major incident at Botany Bay in Kent when his gang ran smack into an ambush. There was a firefight on the beach that March day in 1769 and the smugglers were getting the worst of it. Joss and four men retreated up Kemp's Stairs, killing a Riding Officer. At least four of the smugglers were shot, and legend says that they died of their wounds, with other reports giving the casualties as high as fifteen killed, eight captured and some hanged at Sandwich. Joss survived to die aged ninety-six, full of sin and memories.

The smugglers of Whitstable were another bunch who cared not a toss for king, country or patriotism. If any escaped French prisoner-of-war wished to return home, all he had to do was arrive in Whitstable and promise payment. He would be across the Channel on the next tide, able to resume the fight against perfidious Albion. Jeremiah Curtis, mentioned above, was involved with the Hastings smugglers who called themselves The Transporters or the Hastings Outlaws. Did Richmal Crompton base her *Just William* book on these people?

Overall, there is a strange love of these desperadoes, outlaws and murderers in England. Is it the deeds that command respect? Or is it the daring? It is not only an English thing, for the US film industry has many movies on Jesse James, Billy the kid, Al Capone and the like, but the English seem strangely bent on sanitising the past for the sake of a good folk-hero.

Chapter Fourteen
The Dancers

Most countries have some form of national music or dancing, be they the pipe bands of Scotland, Step Dancing of Ireland or Line Dancing of the United States. Each of those nations can trace the history and story of their traditions. England also has its unique folk dancing.

Nowadays Morris Dancers are a big draw for tourists as well as locals as they jump around with tremendous energy with bells on their trousers, whacking great sticks together. The name itself has obscure origins; it may be derived from Moorish or Morisco, which itself means 'little Moors'. However, there seems no connection between the people of Morocco and the dancers of England.

The earliest reference found so far dates from 1448, so Morris has a relatively long history in England although it may not have originated there. There was a court dance across Europe known as a 'moreys dance' that included bells and fancy costumes, so perhaps it crossed the Channel through trade or diplomacy. It seemed to become sufficiently popular in England to be a fixture in the middle of the sixteenth century, particularly in Church Festivals. Shakespeare mentioned it, so it was obviously well-known by then. Cromwell, not surprisingly, did not approve and banned the practice. When Morris Dancing returned with the Restoration, the costumes had altered to white clothes and bells. There were musicians together with the dancers, originally simple tabor and pipes but gradually joined by all sorts of instruments such as fiddles and accordions as well as a drum.

With industrialisation and the spread of other popular forms of entertainment, Morris Dancing sadly declined in the Victorian age, only to revive with the renewed interest in folk culture in the twentieth century. One of the people who helped retain this strange but traditional form of dancing was Miss Janet Blunt of Oxfordshire. Her father was an officer in the Indian Army who retired to the village of Adderbury in 1892, and she occupied herself by talking to the dancers who had sung the songs their parents and grandparents had taught them. Until Janet Blunt recorded them, the words had been a purely oral tradition and were in danger of being lost.

Even so, the songs and tunes were threatened for when Miss Blunt died; her work would have been tossed into a fire if her sharp-minded former maid had not stepped in to save them. Now the Morris tunes are sung and taught throughout the shire. In Ascott-under-Wychwood, also in Oxfordshire, the annual Hunt used to finish with a display by the Ascott Morris Men. When the Hunt ceased in 1874, the Morris dancers songs began to fade from memory until a gentleman named Reginald Tiddy gathered all he could and revived them again. In 1912 he built Tiddy Hall, which was used as a venue for Morris dancing. In common with so many good men, Reginald Tiddy died in the First World War.

Today Morris Dancing has been re-established across England. A strange but welcome addition to the county's traditional pastimes.

Chapter Fifteen
Springheeled Jack

This character needs a chapter to himself, not only because of the volume of information about him but also because he is unique. Nobody seemed sure if he was a man in a costume, a ghost, a demon a mixture of all three or a hoax. It could have been different people at different times, or a pure fabrication. Springheeled Jack seems to have originated in the latter years of the eighteenth century, and sightings continued on and off until 1995, and will no-doubt re-surface again.

According to legend and story, in the 1770s or 1780s, there was a prankster in the Sheffield area known as the Park Ghost or Spring Heeled Jack. There are few details except that he terrified people and had an extraordinary jumping ability. However, when local vigilantes armed themselves with stout staffs and pistols, Spring Heeled Jack vanished. And that seemed to be the end of that.

However around 1837, Spring Heeled Jack reappeared; this time he was in Surrey and terrorising women, as such creatures of the night tend to do. He materialised at Blackheath Fair and immediately attacked a woman named Polly Adams, grabbing at her Polly's blouse and leaving deep scratches across her midriff. Polly was sure that her attacker had some steel or iron nails on his fingers. At any rate, with his momentary lust satisfied he bounded away again.

Unfortunately in an age before tape recorders and video cameras there is no definite method of recording what occurred, but apparently, Polly Adams reported that her assailant had been Devil-like, although other sources say that she thought he was a pop-eyed nobleman. Polly's was not the only assault; she was only the first of so many that the Lord Mayor had them publicised in an attempt to find the perpetrator. All that happened was a deluge of letters from others who claimed they had also been attacked by a devilish man with spring heels who could bound over walls as if he was a human kangaroo. With Englishmen liking to push themselves to the forefront of events, groups of armed men began to patrol the streets and country lanes, hopeful of finding this bouncing man.

However, they did not catch Jack. Either he bounded away on his spring heels, or the presence of armed patrols frightened him, for the attacks eased and then ended. But not for long; they soon started again in London. Lucy Scales was next to acknowledge that Jack had attacked her and now there was something different. Rather than claw at Miss Scales, Jack spat blue flame at her face.

Miss Scales jerked back, and for a while, she thought she might lose her sight. She recovered and reported the incident. The newspapers spread the news, no doubt supplemented by graphic details supplied by imaginative reporters.

Jack's next recorded victim was Jane Alsop, and once again he altered his method of attack. This time he knocked at Alsop's front door and shouted 'I'm a police officer. For God's sake bring me a light for we've caught Spring Heeled Jack!'

Glad that the reign of fear was now over, Alsop grabbed a lighted candle and handed it to the tall cloaked figure that stood at her gate. He took it and held it close, and Alsop stepped back in shock. Rather than a policeman, the tall figure wore skin tight oilskins, and his eyes glowed red. As in his attack on Lucy Scales, Jack spat blue flame at her then put her in a headlock and ripped at her face and upper body with long talons. Luckily Alsop's sister was at home and rescued her. But Jack was not finished yet. Rather than flee, he continued to hammer at the door as the women screamed for help. He only left when a gaggle of men rushed up the lane to the Alsop household.

For once Spring Heeled Jack left a clue. In his hurry, he dropped his cape, but another man lifted it and also escaped. At least the authorities now knew that Jack did not work alone. The sightings continued with men and women witnessing Jack clambering up a church steeple as handy as any steeple-jack and bounding across rooftops, and then after an abortive attempt to come into a house by the front door, he vanished again.

The country breathed a sigh of relief. There had been speculation on the identity of Jack, with the smart money being on the Marquis of Waterford. His movements were watched carefully and then in 1842 he settled in Ireland with his new wife, just as Jack left England. Perhaps the Marquis had been Jack but if so he must have caught the ferry back across the Irish Sea for next year a whole new spate of Jack-sightings began. This time they were deadly.

For a while, it was the same old story, and then in 1845, Maria Davis was found murdered. She was all of thirteen years old, and popular opinion blamed Jack. Once again Sheffield became the happy hunting ground of Spring Heeled Jack, and the police were on high alert. A red-eyed Jack was seen in Attercliffe, attacking men, groping at women, jumping from rooftop to rooftop and walking erect down walls. The police did not catch him. Nobody could.

Jack's wanderings, or stories about him, spread all over the area, with one sighting leading to another rather in the fashion of UFO or wanted criminals today. He was in the Black Country in the 1850s, Blackheath in the 1870s and Dudley and Birmingham in the 1880s. According to legend and story, the Jack of the 1870s would leap on top of the sentry boxes of army guards, slap them in the face and bound away. Was that true? Or were the young soldiers, bored with the drab routine of barrack life, merely inventing stories to add interest to life.

Jack entered popular literature as a form of anti-hero and sometimes even as a hero. He was the demoniac mischief maker of his day. Always a tall bouncing figure, sometimes with a devilish little beard, a glowing face and a Hispanic appearance, he was never caught. True or not, Spring Heeled Jack became something of a folk legend and parents quietened their children to sleep with the ominous warning that Spring Heeled Jack would get them, much as parents in the North had once warned about the Black Douglas.

Hush ye, hush ye little pet ye
The Black Douglas shall not get ye

Apparently, these mothers had an arrangement with Jack that if the children did not settle down, Jack would bounce up to the window and stare at them with his glowing red eyes.

And then in Netherton in 1877 the police had success. People had seen a man with a single huge eye bounding along beside the canal. As soon as they heard, a body of police rushed to the spot and there he was, a bouncing figure leaping across the canal from bank to bank. They grabbed him, hustled him to the nearest police office and began a detailed interrogation, only to be disappointed. They had caught local man Joseph Darby, a nail maker and collier who was practising to be a spring-jumper by leaping across the canal. The single eye was his miner's helmet. Darby was not Spring Heeled Jack, and later he became the world champion spring jumper and appeared in many competitions. There is a statue of him in Netherton.

The Jack stories continued, dying away for a while only to flare up again. The early suspect, Waterford, had died in 1859 so he was well out of the running, and Jack appeared in Liverpool's William Henry Street in 1904. Then the world altered, wars and depressions and the advent of new technology changed how people lived, and Jack succumbed to the shadows, only to reappear in the 1970s. He made another appearance in 1986 when a man bounced over a hedge in Herefordshire, slapped a retired British officer hard across the face and bounded away. Many Herefordshire roads are bordered by high hedges: Hereford is also the base for the SAS; a military prankster perhaps?

So there is the story, or part of it, of Spring Heeled Jack. What a strange creature he was, with a legend that stretches over two hundred years and outbreaks in various places. Is there a single supernatural bounder? Or was the legend created by a series of copy-cats? Will we even know?

Chapter Sixteen
Going Down The Pub,
Strangely Enough

I mention public houses so often in this book that it seems an excellent idea to have a chapter purely on them. Pubs and inns have been central to English life since at least the Middle Ages, so it would be hard to think of the country, especially the rural parts, without one. This chapter looks at only some of the stories behind a few of the quirky, the unusual and the haunted. Before anybody imagines that I am in any way encouraging readers to imbibe too freely, remember the fate of St Vincent, the patron saint of Drunkards. After refusing to sacrifice to some strange gods, he was martyred on 22nd January 304 by being racked, roasted on a grid-iron and placed, broken and burned, in the stocks until he died.

He may be grateful for the short rhyme that remembers his fatal day:

If on St Vincent the sky be clear
More wine than water will crown the year.

That sounds promising, but I will add one word of warning though. Because of the sad closure of many English country pubs lately, there is, unfortunately, no guarantee that these iconic premises are still open for business. Hopefully, they are and those that have been forced to close re-open soon. The idea of England without public houses does not bear considering.

English pubs were always many and varied; at the beginning of the nineteenth- century, there were an estimated fifty thousand pubs in England, with no fixed closing times. They ranged from filthy one-roomed hovels where 'kill-me-deadly' spirits and diluted ale was slopped out to the dissolute and the destitute, to the gin-parlours that provided gaudy sanctuary from lives of shocking desperation to comfortable inns that gave food and drink of genuine quality.

In the 18th and early nineteenth-century gin was the poison of choice. 'Drunk for a penny, dead drunk for twopence' was the saying and the following lines could be sung to the tune of Home Sweet Home:

Gin, Gin, sweet, sweet Gin
There's no drops like Gin

To many others, beer and ale or even the sharper cider were the drinks of choice of the Englishman or woman. For that, there is no better place in the world than a cosy public house.

English pubs are rarely class-conscious; they will take anybody's money or even their watch. There is a pub in London known as The Castle in Cowcross Street, which King George IV once patronised. The king was a lover of gambling and cockfighting and had lost a lot of money when he combined the two at Clerkenwell. All he had left was a watch, which he took into The Castle to pawn.

Realising with whom he was dealing, the landlord took the watch but returned it to the king the following morning. In return the king allowed the Castle to act as a part-time pawn shop. The name The Castle may seem a little prosaic but pub names often tell their tale. The Romans have the credit for giving pubs names or at least making them more visible, with bars in Rome being marked out by bunches of wine leaves. After invading Britain and spreading the delights of their civilisation, such as baths and slavery, they also built bars and marked them with bunches of foliage from bushes.

The authentic inn did not come to England until the Middle Ages when they were established to care for people on pilgrimage and those who were travelling to the Holy Land. Nottingham has Ye Olde Trip to Jerusalem which has been catering to patrons since 1189 when Richard the Lionheart led his crusade to the Holy Land. This pub has some strange old traditions, such as the Pregnancy Chair for those women who would like a baby. Just sit in it and see what happens – if you dare. There is also a ship in a bottle behind the bar. That is cursed so if you touch it, you die. Naturally, there is also a ghost which haunts a dark passage with the somewhat off-putting name of Mortimer's Hole. In 1330 the energetic King Edward III crawled along this passage from Nottingham Castle to the pub to find Roger Mortimer engaged in some treacherous activity. The unfortunate Mortimer was hanged at Tyburn.

Names such as the Turks Head continued the crusading tradition, while those that portray the Ship could be nautical if they are near the coast, or refer to Noah's Ark if they are inland. Incidentally, the Turk's Head in London was the final watering hole for pirates on their way to execution at Wapping. Perhaps some promised to pay for their rum on their next visit.

Sometimes a pub sign will give a clue as to the derivation of the name. One popular pub name in England is the Marquis of Granby, often showing the Marquis charging with his wig askew. He deserves mention on his own. Born in 1721, John Manners, the Marquis of Granby, was in the army from 1745 until his death in 1770. He was present at the Battle of Culloden, and when his regiment mutinied because the government had forgotten their wages, the marquis paid them from his own money. He was in Flanders in the closing stages of the War of Austrian Succession and during the Seven Years War made a name for his care for the welfare of his men. During the Battle of Warburg, he lost his hat and wig leading a charge –an image that is repeated on many pub signs throughout the country and may be responsible for the saying 'go at them bald-headed.' Overall he was a popular commander and according to tradition, bankrupted himself by buying all his aged non-commissioned officers a public house. He died in debt.

There are many pubs named after the Marquis, including one in Rathbone Street in London where Dylan Thomas and T. S Eliot frequented.

The Smith's Arms in Dorset has its own story, for here Charles II had his horse shod. Being a thirsty as well as a merry monarch, King Charles asked for a tankard of the local beer, only to learn that the smithy did not have a licence. He gave it one there and then and finished his drink without breaking the law.

Indeed there could be an entire book written purely about English pub names, and there probably is. There are many with similar names: Red Lion, Crown, and Royal Oak are relatively standard, but there are others with very distinctive names. Pubs can tell the story of the local area with colour and panache, and a man or woman could do much worse than to tour England by visiting the hostelries, inns and pubs. Some are eye-catching, such as the Jolly Taxpayer in Portsmouth, which is surely an oxymoron. The Nobody Inn in Doddiscombsleigh in Devon is an interesting play on words but also serves as a reminder of the day when the coffin of a long-gone landlord was carried solemnly back to his inn to find it sadly empty.

The Virginia Ash in Henstridge in Wiltshire has a unique past. In 1592 Queen Elizabeth granted Sherborne Castle to Sir Walter Raleigh, one of her most successful piratical sea-dogs. Sir Walter had recently returned from a voyage to the New World and brought with him the amazing discovery of tobacco. It is reported that while he was enjoying a quiet pipe at this inn, the barmaid saw the smoke, thought Raleigh was on fire and emptied a tankard of ale on top of him to douse the flames. Naturally, this old inn is haunted as well.

Buxton in Derbyshire has The Quiet Woman with a pub sign of a headless barmaid carrying a tray. The story goes that a woman named Juthwaire argued with her brother in a local church and he chopped off her head. Not at all happy to have the church looking untidy, the woman lifted her own head and placed it on the altar. That part may be apocryphal; the fact that the decapitated woman now haunts the pub is maybe certain to be true.

York's Three Legged Mare refers to a gallows that can hang three people at once, and the pub has a model gallows in the garden for the curious. Another pub with a grisly hanging reference is the Hung Drawn and Quartered in London's Great Tower Street. In nearby Tower Hill, men were treated in such a barbarous manner in the good old days. Another pub with a grisly name is the Bucket of Blood in Hayle in Cornwall. The story says that a previous landlord drew a bucket from the well to find it full of blood and a butchered body at the bottom of the well. Happy days in Merry England!

Coldharbour in London's Isle of Dogs has a public-house with the short and succinct name of The Gun. The building dates back to the early eighteenth-century, and the establishment is still going strong. The name harks back to 1802 when a cannon was fired to announce the opening of the West India Import Dock, but there is much more nautical history.

As well as smugglers who had a spy-hole in the wall so they could watch for Excise men, Admiral Nelson was a regular visitor. When not at sea the one-armed, one-eyed admiral lived nearby and often popped in when he was inspecting the ships in the docks. Tradition claims that Nelson and Lady Hamilton met in the River Room upstairs to do whatever admirals and their lovers do on these occasions.

Stalybridge in Tameside has two pubs with names worth mentioning. One is the Q Inn, which is said to be the shortest pub name in England; the other is The Old Thirteenth Cheshire Astley Volunteer Rifleman Corps Inn, which has the reputation of being the longest name. Imagine the embarrassment of phoning for a taxi to take you home and trying to remember a name of such length.

Outside Plymouth University is the Skiving Scholar, which is an excellent name for a place that will undoubtedly be a haunt for students who would be better employed in their studies.

Another pub with a great name and an even more significant history is the Prospect of Whitby in Wapping, London. The infamous Judge Jeffries used to be a patron as he stuffed himself with good food and watched the executioner hang condemned men across the river at Execution Dock. This spot was where many pirates bade farewell to the world. They were hanged at low tide and left as an exhibition until three tides had passed over their sad corpses.

The pub itself dates back to 1520, making it London's most historic Thames-side drinking establishment, with smugglers and generations of interesting people drank here. Charles Dickens, Samuel Pepys and Kirk Douglas were only three of the patrons.

A happy little name with a unique story is the Drunken Duck in Ambleside. An earlier landlady came home and was shocked to find that all her prized ducks were lying dead. Momentarily nonplussed, she decided that the best thing to do was to cook them, so she plucked them one by and laid them aside ready to put in the oven. However the last duck she plucked revived, and the others showed signs of stirring she realised that they were dead drunk rather than merely dead. There was a leaking beer barrel in the yard, and the ducks had been imbibing rather too deeply. According to legend, the kindly landlady felt so sorry for the featherless ducks that she knitted each a smart little jacket to keep it warm.

In Beaconsfield, Buckinghamshire, the Crown Inn has a charming little tale. A highwayman named Claude Duval patronised the Crown, and on one occasion he was having a quiet tankard when he overheard a farmer talking. The farmer boasted to all and sundry that he had made £100 profit from the Beaconsfield Fair. Now that was too good an opportunity to miss, but how could he separate the burly farmer from his gains?

Simple: enlist the help of the devil. Duval had a little word or two with one of the drinkers, and within a short time, the devil appeared, sliding down the flue of the chimney complete with rough skin and a horned head. As the patrons fled from the Inn in gibbering fear, Duval neatly removed the farmer's cash-bag. He slipped from the Inn and a short time later met his confederate who had donned the cow's horns and cowhide and paid him his share of the loot.

The Royal Anchor Hotel in Hampshire's Liphook had a slightly less sinister patron in a highwayman known as Captain Jacques who ensured the road to Portsmouth was lively for travellers. He used the Royal Anchor's hidden rooms and secret openings to his advantage. However, on one occasion he failed to open a secret door inside a fireplace, and that was the end of Captain Jacques.

Glastonbury's High Street has the George and Pilgrim Hotel, which has stood there since 1475. Rather than highwaymen, there are two closely related ghosts as a young and well-dressed woman follows a monk who wanders the corridors in the dim hours of early morning. The story goes that they were lovers in everything but the physical, so are doomed to remain in the hotel through their unconsummated love.

Ghosts, thievery and inns seemed to be bound by some unholy alliance. In sixteenth-century Buckinghamshire, a gentleman named John Jarman was the landlord of The Ostrich at Colnbrook. He was as unpleasant a man as any in the country, and travellers were best to avoid his establishment and steer clear of his ale.

In common with many inns, Jarman brewed his own ale and had a guest room right above his brewery. His house also had some unique features, such as a bed in that room that was securely fastened to the floor and had a mattress attached. Much worse was the hinged trap door in the floor beneath the bed. If Jarman believed that his guest had anything worth stealing, he could slip into the Brewhouse, slide back the bolts so the trap door opened and the guest would slide straight into the boiling vat of ale. The body, often burned beyond recognition, was then tipped into the nearby river and floated away.

With the visitor safely deceased, Jarman and his charming wife would take all his money and anything else of value. Then there was the patron's horse; it was simple enough to trim the tail and cut the mane before selling it to a shady horse dealer. The Ostrich ran this profitable side-business for quite some time before things started to go wrong. One of the sixty or so dead bodies he had tossed into the river snagged on a tree and did not float away; it washed up on the river bank and was recognised. There were questions asked at the Inn, and the Jarmans were soon before the beak. The hangman stretched their necks.

Of course, there are variations on the story to this inn, which sits not far from Heathrow. One version says the murders were committed as far back as the twelfth century, which was a few hundred years before the pub was built - although these are legends of a mediaeval hospice on the same site. Another gives the actual words that John Jarman spoke to his wife:

'There is a fat pig to be had if you want one.'

If she agreed, she would reply: 'I pray you put him in the hogsty till tomorrow' and then Jarman tipped the victim into a vat of boiling water rather than ale. Unfortunately for tradition, the tale seems to be based on an old novel rather than on historical fact, but the author of the novel possibly based it on a local legend that itself could be true... Stranger and stranger. Add to that the possibility that the original story may have been re-used in the Sweeny Todd Demon Barber idea and things get even more attractive.

Sometimes breweries could be as dangerous as any murderous landlord. In October 1814 a fermentation tank in the Horse Shoe Brewery in London's Tottenham Court Road burst, with the force rupturing other vats and then smashing down the brick wall of the building. Over three hundred thousand gallons of beer gushed into the local area, the St Giles rookery in a fifteen-foot-high wave. This surge of beer killed six people and injured many others; it badly damaged the Tavistock Arms and trapped an unfortunate barmaid inside. There were also reports of another death as a man drank too much of this free beer.

Indeed scores of people rushed to the scene with pots and pails and tankards, or even just their cupped hands, to imbibe what they could before the flood dissipated. Happy days for all except the casualties.

Another Inn with an unpleasant landlord stood near to St Neots in Cambridgeshire, where mine host stole from those guests who were worth his attention. In those seventeenth or eighteenth-century days it was not uncommon for guests to have to share a bed, so when he had three fairly well off men in one bed, he murdered them all in one bloody night, dragged their bodies to a well and tossed them in. However, justice was done when the murderer was discovered and hung on the nearest gibbet.

Of course, most pubs are far more pleasant today. Sometimes country pubs even have mummers to entertain the clientele around Christmas time. For those who do not know, mummers perform silent plays- mum means silent, hence the expression to keep mum – with a simple plot of good versus evil.

Chard in Somerset has the Choughs Hotel, which was built in the seventeenth century and has a fascinating history. In its time it has been a school and a brothel, either of which establishments could create enough trauma for a dozen ghosts. One of the saddest of spirits is young Elizabeth who lives – if that is the correct word- in a first-floor bedroom. In 1845, with her mother and sister both prostitutes, she poisoned herself rather than share their lifestyle.

A second bedroom was the scene of a murder when a man was stabbed to death, and the attic holds the ghost of a hanging man as well as a poltergeist unless they are the same spirit. The bar also has its share of spirits, and not all are in the optics, with unearthly people wandering around and a dead elderly couple enjoying a quiet drink together.

A Grey Lady haunts the Old Bell Hotel at Malmesbury in Wiltshire. The hotel itself was said to have foundations stretching back to 1220, while people claim that the east wing is built on the graveyard of the abbey next door. Naturally, that could lead to tales of ghosts, bogles and things that go drifting in the night, although from where the Grey Lady comes is anybody's guess. Perhaps she just seeks the company of this friendly establishment. The Grey Lady inhabits the James Ody Room, although to judge by her melancholic appearance she does not entirely approve of her surroundings. If one wishes to summon her, just say 'Grey Lady' three times in her room and wait.

While the Lady is benign if hardly cheerful, the entity in the Danvers Room is slightly more active, tossing guests' possessions around the room or hauling off the covers in the dark. On at least one occasion something blocked the entrance to the Foe Room by dragging a wardrobe across the door. Augmenting the pub's atmosphere is the legend of sarcophagi hidden under the bar.

Sharing the same name and the haunted reputation, the Old Bell Pub in Gloucester's Southgate Street is much more modern, dating from the seventeenth century. It has a spirit that remains in the gentleman's toilets (strange place to choose) and a poltergeist named Elsie. Now known as the Tiger's Eye restaurant, at one time the building was used as a courthouse, and rough justice was not unknown with innocent men reportedly sent to the gallows. Some of them are believed to have remained to protest at their untimely demise.

Many people may remember the name Henry Higgins as the professor in *Pygmalion*, filmed as *My Fair Lady*. The author may have filched the name from another elegant man of the same name, a Henry Higgins who rose high in the upper echelons of society in Knutsford in Cheshire. One of his haunts was a coaching inn called the Royal George, which had Assembly Room for balls and soirees as well as numerous bars.

This particular Henry Higgins bowed to and flattered the belles in the Assembly Rooms, then made an excuse, backed away and slipped into the lady's powder room and took whatever he fancied before returning to the dancing. Not only that, but Higgins was also a highwayman. Preferring moonlight to darkness, he would slide a thick sock over the hooves of his horse and set out with pistol and mask, with burglary added to his list of talents whenever he had the notion.

The executioner hanged him in November 1767, but his memory and his ghost survive in his house beside the Heath. As Eliza Doolittle would have said:

> *Just you wait, 'Enry 'Iggins, just you wait*
> *You'll be sorry, but your tears'll be too late.*

The Ragged Cot Inn at Minchinhampton in Gloucestershire has a reputation for good food and strange noises. Once again there was a highwayman involved: the combination of inns and highwaymen seems to be another English tradition. In December 1760 the landlord of the Ragged Cot was Bill Clavers, and either his accounts were not as he wished or he had a taste for adventure for he decided he should hold up the London stage. He does not seem to have been an experienced highwayman so fortified himself with half a bottle of rum before he set off.

A drunken landlord is perhaps not the best person to leave in charge of a loaded pistol, and sober Mrs Clavers tried to dissuade Bill from his intended robbery. Not in full control of himself, Clavers pushed her away and his wife, holding their young child, slipped and fell head first down the stairs.

Ignoring her, Clavers staggered onto his horse and swayed away through a flurry of snow to meet the coach. Despite his cargo of drink, Clavers managed to successfully rob the coach and rode home in triumph to tell his wife. He entered the Ragged Coat, only to see his wife and child lying where he had left them, crumpled and lifeless at the bottom of the stairs.

Still suffering from the effects of the rum, Clavers was unsure what to do. Seeing a trunk close by, he lifted the lid and stuffed the dead bodies inside.

In the meantime, the driver of the coach had reported the robbery to the authorities, who had dispatched a couple of local constables to investigate. Their job was easier than usual as they could see the hoof-prints of Clavers' horse in the snow. The constables followed the prints to the Ragged Cot and banged imperiously on the door. Not surprisingly, given the events of the evening, Clavers did not reply.

As the constables smashed through the shutters and opened a window, Clavers aimed and fired his pistol, with the ball going nowhere. The leading constable lifted his gun but before he fired Clavers began to scream. He saw his dead wife and child floating just above the ground as they crossed the hall and ascended the stairs as they had only a few hours before.

Still in shock, Clavers dropped his pistol and surrendered meekly to the constables. Tying him to a chair, they searched the inn for the proceeds from the coach robbery. Instead, they met the ghost of Mrs Clavers sitting on the chest in which her body was concealed. Leaving Clavers tied to his chair, the constables ran. Returning in daylight, they opened the trunk and found Mrs Clavers and the child inside. A jury found Clavers guilty of the coach robbery and of killing his wife and baby. He was hanged, but the ghost of his wife remains in the pub.

England's pubs and inns, then, can provide just about anything from tales of highwaymen to animals to a host of ghost stories. They are the focal points for a thousand communities, the base for sports and the centre of life. Drop in and enjoy!

Chapter Seventeen
A Strange Day Out

Merry old England could be a very violent place. High-waymen and highwaywomen infested the roads to such an extent that in some stretches they virtually queued up to rob travellers; footpads lurked in the streets of cities and towns, the fairs were the haunt of pickpockets, scoundrels and bands of foot-loose wanderers while smugglers and wreckers lived along the coast. There were political riots, religious riots, anti-improvement riots, Luddite riots, bread riots, king's birthday riots and riots to celebrate military victories. The Army and Navy maintained discipline with the lash, with some enthusiastic floggers such as the Duke of Kent or Captain Bligh of HMS *Bounty* bringing men to the brink of mutiny or beyond. Add the bloody pastimes of bear baiting, ratting, cockfighting, hare-coursing, fox-hunting and bare-knuckle pugilism, and the populace savoured gore. Given such a lifestyle, it was not surprising that the pleasures of the people were not at all what people of today would expect. Rather than one of the most polite countries in the world, Olde England was seeped in blood and cruelty.

One frequent form of free entertainment was a public execution. Any hanging would attract a crowd, while the hanging of a known personality such as a notorious murderer or highwayman could bring out tens of thousands of interested spectators. There were said to be around two hundred thousand people at the execution of Jack Sheppard, a famous criminal in his time and when the highwayman Claude Duval graced Tyburn in January 1670, much of the crowd who wept for him was female.

One of the best-remembered hanging spots in England, if not in the world was at Tyburn in London. The first recorded execution here was in 1196 although there may well have been some before that. The name is from the Tye or Teo Bourne or Burn, meaning Boundary Stream. Rather than the standard single scaffold, from 1571 the Tyburn gallows was triangular, known as the Triple Tree and was placed at the intersection of three different parishes, St Marylebone, Paddington and St George's. There is a circular plaque marking the spot now, not far from Marble Arch.

Being the capital city of England, London tended to attract the nation's criminals as well as the elite and the ambitious on whom they preyed. To cope with the constant influx of unwanted, the Tyburn Tree could execute up to twenty-four criminals at any one time, which must have been a sight fit to shock anybody except the most brazen. The original gallows, or at least an earlier version, collapsed in 1678, allegedly torn down by the ghosts of those who had ended their lives hanged here. The triple gallows survived until 1783 and was in frequent use.

There were twelve hanging days a year and John Taylor the Water Poet immortalised the Tyburn Tree in verse:

> *I have heard sundry men oft times dispute*
> *Of trees, that in one year will twice bear fruit.*
> *But if a man note Tyburn, 'will appear,*
> *That that's a tree that bears twelve times a year.*

There was so much interest that hanging days were public holidays for the lower classes who lined the streets from the jail at Newgate to the gallows at Tyburn. Perhaps the idea was to terrify potential criminals into walking the straight and narrow, but to most folk, it was merely a pleasant day out watching the demise of others. The bell of St Sepulchre only tolled when there was to be a hanging, summoning people to attend the scene. Standing in the back of a cart, the condemned was accompanied by the hangman and prison chaplain, while soldiers ensured there was no attempt at a rescue. The route was through Holborn and St Giles and along what is now Oxford Street – what would today's wealthy shoppers think of that?

At the triple-tree, the more loquacious of the condemned could speak to the crowd, thus starting a tradition that is continued in nearby Speaker's Corner even today. There were two central characters to this terminal drama: the man or woman who was about to bid farewell and the headsman, the executioner.

The role of executioner was one that attracted considerable publicity, and England had some prominent characters, not least Jack Ketch, whose name became the generic term for every man who subsequently occupied that position.

After the Restoration of King Charles II, it was wise to remain religiously orthodox within the Church of England. Anything else was liable to lead to pointing fingers and could finish with the Tyburn jig or the Tower. The final official in the chain of prosecution was Jack Ketch, who turned off traitors, murderers and anybody else to whom authority took a fatal dislike.

Nobody is certain when Ketch was born, or where, or what his real name was. He may have been John Ketch or Jack Catch and could have been Irish or English. What is known about him is not pleasant. Parents used his name as a bogey-man to encourage their wayward children to behave:

'Keep quiet, or Jack Ketch will get you.'

Historians believe that Jack Ketch lived in the Grey's Inn Road area in London and was married to a woman named Katherine, and he worked as public executioner from 1666 to 1678. They also know that he was frequently drunk when he worked and was always avaricious. One of the perks of the job was to keep the clothes of the condemned, which does not sound particularly lucrative, except that men liked to look good on their final farewell and wore their best. In the case of successful highwaymen or members of the nobility that could mean silks and satins which would fetch a high price in a pawn shop or as mementoes to those of the public who liked a grisly souvenir. Add to that the traditional gift that victims could hand to the executioner to ensure that their end was speedy and relatively painless and Mr Ketch should have been at least comfortably well off.

Ketch did not only hang people, but he also decapitated some and had the bloody job of drawing and quartering others – taking out their bowels and cutting up the bodies. He would place the heads on public display on Tower Bridge or other prominent sites. It was also Ketch's job to plunge executed prisoners in boiling pitch before displaying them on gibbets. He did this at Newgate Prison, a place of pain and despair that now gained another title: Jack Ketch's kitchen. The original Jack Ketch died in 1686, but the name lived on.

Until well into the nineteenth century, public executions were the norm in England. Often they attracted a crowd of thousands including women and children, balladeers, broadsheet sellers, hot-pie sellers and a host of pick-pockets to augment the stalls and banter. A good hanging would be spoken about for days, much as a good football match is today.

However, Tyburn was not the only execution spot in London. Traitors said their final farewell at Tower Hill, pirates at Wapping's Execution Dock, heretics, witches and wives who murdered their husbands swung at West Smithfield, and thieves who worked the Thames at East Smithfield. There were other execution sites including St. Pauls and Smithfield.

The body could often be taken away and used for public dissection to teach a new generation of anatomists, while some human ghouls often retained pieces of the rope as treasured mementoes. There was much more: a cloth dipped in the condemned man's sweat could be used to heal sickness, and some desperate people believed that they could cure their illnesses by touching the hanged man in the equivalent part of his anatomy. It was not unknown for some person of strong nerves to partially flay the deceased later and use the skin for various purposes.

The dead man's hand was the most valuable of all. If a burglar wished to be invisible, all he or she had to do was to obtain the hand of a hanged man, have it mummified and burn a candle on top. To be fully effective, the candle had to be made either of human fat or the combined fats of a bear, an unbaptised child and a badger; put all together and the result would be a 'hand of glory'. It is unclear how many burglars used this method as they would be invisible.

In some cases, the executioner hanged criminals in gibbets, a sort of iron cage where they were left to rot or their bones to be picked clean by birds and insects.

In one case on Wardlaw Mires in Derbyshire, a murderer named Anthony Lingard swung from the gallows. It was 1812, and he had killed a widow who ran a tollgate. As soon as he died, the executioner gibbetted his corpse. Hosts of ghouls gathered to stare at his slowly decomposing body rather than attending church, so the local vicar held his Sunday services in the shadow of the executed man. Remembering that the Romans executed Christ, the site of the sermon may be more fitting than it initially sounds. In 1767 a man named Thomas Nicholson was gibbetted at Beacon Hill in Penrith. Although the actual body is long gone, his ghost remains in the form of a skeleton, with the wind howling between his naked bones.

The hideous practice of gibbeting probably began in the reign of King Henry III in the thirteenth century and was intended to act as a deterrent to others. The gibbet was positioned at a prominent place such as a crossroads or beside the gate into a town as a cheerful reminder of the fate of ne'er- do-wells. With the bodies often covered in tar, passing travellers would have to endure the grisly scene for weeks at a time. Often the uprights were of iron, as relatives of the deceased would saw down wooden gibbets to give the unfortunate occupant a Christian burial, without which he was condemned to forever wander the earth. Gibbetting ended in 1834, no doubt to the relief of travellers of tender susceptibilities.

With so many hangings, modern readers may think that old England was a place where a murder was an everyday event. However, capital punishment was not just for murder but for a whole host of offences. At one time there were two hundred and twenty ways in which to get oneself hanged including impersonating a Chelsea Pensioner, roaming at night with a blackened face or even damaging Westminster Bridge. One needed to be very careful in the strange old days.

Hounslow Heath was another cheerful place for robbery with violence, a sort of Highwayman Central. The authorities decided to brighten the location with a whole row of gibbets to daunt the gentlemen of the pad. It did not discourage anybody, of course, and one murky night a company of axemen came along and chopped the whole lot down.

Some crimes live in the public memory even to this day. One which is still annually celebrated occurred in 1606 when Guy Fawkes and his gang of friends tried to blow up the king and parliament. They failed, and the result was a rash of executions including that of Everard Digby. He was a handsome sort of fellow and was sentenced to be hanged, drawn and quartered. The hanging part was bad enough, stringing a man up by his neck, so he choked and kicked and spun at the end of a rope, but then the authorities cut him down before he died. The next phase was worse, lying the victim face up on a block to be sliced open and his innards drawn out. According to legend, the executioner cracked open Digby's ribs and hauled out his heart with the traditional 'Here is the heart of a traitor', but Digby had the last word as he shouted out 'thou liest' and promptly expired again. Not many dead men could speak like that.

Not only executions attracted the crowds; other punishments could also be barbarically entertaining, such as whipping a man or woman through the streets or placing them in the stocks. The latter could be painful and humiliating, sitting with one's legs trapped within a substantial wooden framework, open to the ridicule and missiles of a hostile mob. The stocks were in use in the Oxfordshire village of Aston Rowant in the middle of the sixteenth century when some imprudent bellringers rang their bells to honour Princess Elizabeth when her captors took her through the village on her journey to imprisonment in Rycote.

Another Oxfordshire person, Hannah Graves, spent time in the Begbroke stocks in 1723 when she was caught disturbing the peace of the village. Her husband, John Graves, landlord of the Royal Sun, was fined a whopping £40 for a similar offence.

Then there was the pillory when the culprit had to stand facing the mob with his or her face and hands pinioned by a solid wooden framework. As well as abuse and ridicule, the offender could often face a hail of objects. In

July 1810 Edward Roberts and Dorothy Cole were pilloried at Charing Cross and according to the *Newgate Calendar* were 'severely pelted with rotten eggs and all manner of filth... Until they bore little resemblance of human beings.' The pillory was not a mild punishment.

Some punishments were worse than the stocks or the noose. England had a shocking method of convincing the accused to plead either guilty or innocent. If men refused to plead, the law subjected them to the terrible ordeal of being pressed to death. The law ordained that the prisoner was taken to a dark room, stripped almost naked and spread-eagled on the ground and 'there shall be laid upon his body as much iron or stone as he can bear, and more'. As the weights slowly crushed the malefactor to death, he was allowed 'three morsels of barley bread' the first day, stagnant water and no bread the second day and so on until he dies or agreed to plead.

Sometimes the prisoner in jail had his own way of fooling the authorities. For instance, when John Bunyan was imprisoned, he entertained himself by playing on the flute. The turnkeys did not approve of a prisoner being happy, so they searched his cell for the flute but without any success. Bunyan disguised his flute as one of the back struts of his chair, simple yet effective.

The final person featured in this gruesome chapter will be Ann Green. She was no noblewoman or great benefactor, and not even a ghost. Instead, she was just an ordinary woman, a maid at Duns Tew Manor in Oxfordshire. In 1650 she was taken to the local assizes when somebody found her dead baby hidden in the manor where she worked.

During the trial, her story came out. The baby's father was the son of the Lord of the Manor, Sir Thomas Read, so was Ann's master. He had pushed himself on Ann time and again until he threatened her with losing her position unless she agreed to have sex. With no choice, she had reluctantly assented and fell pregnant. Despite arguing that the baby was still-born, Ann was found guilty of murder and duly hanged in Oxford Castle Yard.

As was sometimes the custom, her relations were loath to see her suffer slow strangulation so took hold of her legs and pulled her down to kill her more quickly. Ann hung for thirty agonising minutes before she was cut down and handed to the local saw-bones for dissection.

Stripped naked and placed on the slab, Ann lay there, face up as Dr William Petty sharpened his scalpel and prepared to slice her open. He started as he thought he saw her chest move as if she was still breathing. Investigating further, he realised Ann was still alive and encouraged her until she recovered completely. Having already been hanged, Ann could not be executed a second time and was later pardoned. She left her village for one a few miles away, married and had three children.

That upbeat story is a good place to leave this brief look at one of England's strangest entertainments-watching the execution of other people.

Chapter Eighteen
The Strange Tale of a
Disappearing Time Slip

In common with most European countries, England sent thousands of men to fight in the Crusades, the Holy Wars of the Middle Ages when Christendom struggled to regain the Holy Land from Islam. In 1364 the time the forces of Islam in Egypt were planning an attack on the Christian kingdom of Cyprus, so King Peter I of Cyprus called for help from all over Europe. There is an alternative theory that Peter I wanted to replace Alexandria with Famagusta in Cyprus as a major economic centre for the Eastern Mediterranean. Sir Edward Estur from the Isle of Wight was one of the Christian knights who sailed eastward to help defend Cyprus.

Sir Edward did not travel alone. His sweetheart, Lucy Lightfoot from near Carisbrooke Castle in Wight, was at his side. She was a bright, active young woman and as brave as any knight. The pair joined the Christian forces as they assembled at Rhodes, the then headquarters of the Knights of St John, but although Lucy wished to go and fight alongside Sir Edward, he persuaded her to wait for him. She only agreed when Sir Edward promised to marry her on his return.

Knowing that Sir Edward would keep his word, Lucy watched the Christian fleet sail away with her man on board. As it vanished over the horizon, she sighed, sailed to Cyprus and knew she had to resign herself to an interminably long wait. In the meantime, Sir Edward was fighting the Saracens and Mamelukes. The armies of Islam were formidable enemies, technologically and tactically more advanced than the Christians and far outnumbering them. Only in bravery and endurance were the Christians a match.

The Christian army landed at Alexandria in October 1365, defeated the defenders and sacked the city. Apparently, they made a diversionary attack on the west, and when the defenders fought there, another force landed in the east and took the Mamelukes armies in the rear. With the Mamelukes defeated the Crusaders sacked Alexandria and took thousands of slaves. Sir Edward was prominent in the fighting and then joined an ancillary expedition to raid northward along the coast of the Levant. Somewhere in this campaign he was involved in a skirmish with the Saracens and took a sword slash to the head. Such wounds are dangerous even now and much more so then. Sir Edward was severely sick for months, and when he recovered, he had lost part of his memory. He could not remember Rhodes or Cyprus or even Lucy. A kindly ship carried him home to England, leaving Lucy alone in Cyprus.

According to one story, Lucy waited for years and then, believing Sir Edward dead, married a local fisherman.

However, the story does not end there. It would hardly be strange if it did. Nearly five hundred years later, in the year 1831, a seventeen-year-old woman with the name of Lucy Lightfoot was drawn to the church of St Olave's in Gatcombe in the Isle of Wight.

She entered and found a carved oaken effigy of Sir Edward Estur inside. There was nothing out of the ordinary about Lucy; she lived at Gatcombe with her father and two sisters and had never heard about the crusades, but once she saw that effigy she was drawn to it again and again. Sir Edward's effigy had his dog at his feet and a lodestone in the hilt of the sword that had done so much work in the East.

And then at about half-past ten on the 13th June 1831, Lucy entered St Olave's church for the last time. It was a foul day of teeming rain, with thunder growling and grumbling across the sky and flashes of lightning flickering behind the summer trees. As there was also an eclipse, it was a perfect day for a gothic horror story, and that is exactly as it seemed when Lucy vanished, never to be seen again.

All across Wight, people cowered indoors waiting for the weather to abate. When the storm passed and the skies cleared, somebody asked where Lucy was. They found her horse tethered to the church gate, but there was no sign of her. The effigy of St Edward was in place, but the lodestone in the sword hilt was missing, and a steel misericord had shattered to pieces, possibly by a lightning strike. Naturally, there was a search, and Lucy's parents offered a reward. There was nothing.

Now, this is where the theorists have had a field day. Some have said that the combination of an electric storm with an eclipse, together with the force of love that crossed centuries came together when a bolt of lightning struck the lodestone and created a slip in the timeline. Lucy was transported back to mediaeval Cyprus to be with her knightly lover. That is an interesting theory and reads much better than the pragmatic story that the Reverent James Evans, vicar of St Olave's made the whole story up in the 1960s to raise funds.

Now that would be strange, a holy man lying in print to make money.

So was it the time slip or the money-making scam? Hopefully the former although the latter is the more likely.

Chapter Nineteen
A Chapter of Horrors

England has been the venue for many battles. There were battles between the British tribes and the Romans and battles between the British kingdoms and the invading Anglo-Saxons. There were battles when the Anglo-Saxons fought each other and battles where they fought the Vikings and Danes. There was a hard-fought battle against the Normans and encounters with Welsh and Scots. Then there were the civil wars when the English slaughtered each other in fraternal rivalry, with a king, protector or some other opportunistic ruler benefitting from the blood of thousands of probably better and braver men.

One battle that historians rarely mention is Sedgemoor. This savage encounter was fought on the 6th July 1685 when the Duke of Monmouth, the illegitimate son of Charles II and Lucy Walter, tried to usurp the less-than-popular King James VII and II.

By 1685 Monmouth was already a veteran soldier, having fought in Europe and Scotland. He was also a Protestant when the contemporary King James was a Catholic and at a time when religious divides tore the country apart.

In June 1685, Monmouth's rebellion began. Gathering a small army of only eighty-one followers, the Duke landed at Lyme Regis in Dorset and soon whistled up another three hundred. With less than four hundred men mustered in a remote part of the country, it was an uncanny foretaste of the much more famous rising of Prince Charles Edward Stuart in Scotland some sixty years later and with much the same aim: to gain the throne of the United Kingdom. The only difference was that in this case, a Stuart sat on the throne.

Monmouth led his ragged army northward, attracting men by the day, but rather than seasoned soldiers they were peasants and farm servants. By July he had some three thousand would-be-soldiers and had experienced a few skirmishes with those who supported King James. Rather than a warm July, the army was scourged by rain and high winds. Eventually, they reached the town of Bridgewater. Here in deepest Somerset, they entrenched and made ready for a Royalist attack.

Elsewhere, the Rising had not gone well. The Royal Navy had captured the tiny rebel navy, and the Royal Scottish Army had squashed Argyll's ancillary rebellion in Scotland. Monmouth's few thousand men were all alone, and James's soldiers were approaching. Perhaps that news filtered through to the soldiers, who began to drift away in small numbers.

Rather than sit tight and defend Bridgewater, where his men had the advantage of sheltering walls, Monmouth decided to march out to meet the Royal army in the open field. Again in a manner so similar to the prelude to Culloden, Monmouth led his men in a night march across the marshy, wet Somerset moors.

Toiling, exhausted, ill-armed, Monmouth's men staggered on, falling into one drainage ditch after another and making enough noise to alert the devil or even an opposing army. A royal patrol heard them, and Monmouth lost his chance of surprise.

On the 6th July 1685, the two armies met in the last battle in Southern England. It was very one-sided as the professional redcoats of James's army made mincemeat of Monmouth's farm servants and hopeful volunteers. There were around two thousand men killed and the survivors, plus any locals who may have supported Monmouth were rounded up for judgement. That was when an already sordid affair turned into something like a horror movie.

With the battle won, Colonel Percy Kirke was ordered to pacify the West. Kirke was a veteran of Tangier where he led his regiment, known as Kirke's Lambs because of the paschal lamb it bore as regimental insignia. Kirke already had a reputation for ferocity, and he decorated the trees of Somerset with the hanging bodies of dead rebels, while the White Hart Inn in Taunton was similarly blessed. According to local lore, Kirke had his fifers and trumpeters playing merry tunes while his victims struggled and died within their hempen nooses.

As kings traditionally hanged, drew and quartered traitors, legend has Kirke hacking the executed into pieces and employing a local man nicknamed Tom Boilman who plunged the mutilated bodies into vats of pitch. Karma caught Boilman later, for a lightning strike frizzled him as he sheltered beneath an oak tree. The combination of divine retribution and the sacred oak is interesting, if probably untrue. King James later recalled Kirke, not because he was too severe but because he accepted bribes to allow the wealthy to walk free. Such indulgence was not to be allowed: everybody should suffer if they turned against the king.

As Tolkien said: *A King will have his way in his own hall, be it folly or wisdom.*

The king need not have worried about leniency. Justice was riding west in the shape of Judge Jeffries, backed by five others of his ilk. Sir Robert Wright; Sir William Montague; Sir Francis Wytherns, Sir Creswell Levinz and Sir Henry Polexfen jostled to the West Country to exact the king's justice if never his mercy.

Jeffries became notorious for his implacable decisions that veered between straightforward executions to transportation to the American colonies. History can only be grateful that one man who escaped the sweeping was named Daniel Defoe, the future spy and novelist.

George Jeffreys, 1st Baron Jeffreys of Wem was a Welsh-born, English-educated career lawman. His father supported the king when the Civil War started and slipped stealthily to the winning side when Charles' star began to fade; he picked whichever side was best suited to his career. Young George Jeffries endured a single year at Cambridge before joining the Law at the Inner Temple. He had two wives, both enlarging his purse, which argues for marriage-for-profit rather than any notion of romance. Anne, his second wife, was a bad-tempered woman, so the pair was known as St George and his dragon; she seemed a fitting partner to the slippery, career conscious, brutal man that was Judge Jeffries.

Although a Protestant, Jeffreys worked for the Catholic King James VII and II and still managed to persecute those who took part in the Popish Plot: in fact, he would do anything that advanced the interests of George Jeffreys.

In the 1670s, a Rutlandshire priest and Cambridge failure named Titus Oates created the fiction of the Popish Plot to overthrow King Charles II that had people in England searching for Catholics under-the-bed and everywhere else. Oates has gone down in history as Titus the Liar and was surely one of the most repulsive men of his time, matching Kirke and even Jeffreys himself for sheer nastiness. A one-time Royal Navy chaplain, Oates was dismissed for homosexual offences that could have seen him hanged, but his clerical status saved him. In a complex life that saw him veer between the Protestant and Catholic faiths, Oates and a man named Israel Tonge created a purely fictitious Jesuit plot to murder King Charles II. Twenty-two men died because of Oates's perjuries. Jeffreys worked with Oates, accepted his glibly false evidence and hanged men accordingly.

When the throw of the dice put James VII and II on the throne in 1685, the new king called Oates to trial and Jeffries was there to judge a man with whom he had previously worked. Jeffreys was equally happy to insult Oates, call him a 'shame to mankind' and sentence him to be whipped through the streets of London five times a year for the rest of his life. This same Judge Jeffreys was now set loose on the hard-used people of the West Country.

With his headquarters at Taunton, Jeffreys he began a series of trials that became known as the Bloody Assizes earned him the sobriquet of the Hanging Judge. Jeffreys moved from town to town; he sentenced thirteen men to be hanged in Dorchester on his first day, while scores of others were hanged, flogged, jailed or sold into slavery. In Taunton alone, Jeffreys condemned a hundred and forty-four men to death. Heads and body parts of the executed decorated crossroads, village greens and marketplaces and the sickening aroma of death hung like a terrible cloud over the roads and byways of the West. Of those sentenced to transportation, about twenty percent died before they got to their destination, twice the percentage of the slave-ships.

Rather than the impartial judge, Jeffreys was said to laugh and joke his way through his hanging sessions. Perhaps he was drunk. Perhaps he merely enjoyed his job. When Jeffreys informed King James of the progress of the trials the Earl of Sunderland, the Secretary of State, confirmed that his Majesty approved of the slaughter and torture of his subjects.

One man, twenty-four-year-old John Tutchin, was convicted of stating that Hampshire supported the Duke of Monmouth. Jeffreys ordered that the public executioner periodically whip Tutchin through every market town of Devon for the next seven years. As it happened, Tutchin caught smallpox in prison, and kind hands freed him. Jeffries also sentenced a female innkeeper to be whipped through every market town in Dorset and a fifteen-year-old boy was given a similar sentence. He sent eight-year-old girls to prison and sold hundreds into a decade of slavery. The list of horrors is sickening and seems never-ending.

The figures vary, but Jeffreys ordered around two hundred people to be hanged, with a further eight hundred sent to the West Indies, which was a virtual prolonged death sentence due to the harsh labour and tropical diseases. Other sources lower the number of executed to one hundred and fifty. Naturally, such a series of brutal events has left a legacy of ghosts and stories of hauntings.

Westonzoyland, a village and parish in the Somerset Levels, has a story of ghostly sounds, with the patter of running feet coinciding with the clopping of a horse. The legend says that government soldiers captured one of Monmouth's followers here and Kirke's Lambs found out that he had a reputation of being a fast runner. That gave them the idea for a little game; let him race a horse from a standing start. If he won, then he would escape with his life. If he lost, then it was a hempen noose and a drop from the branch of a tree.

Running for his life, the young man won the race. Perhaps he looked too triumphant, or maybe the Lambs had no intention of setting him free, for they hanged or shot him despite his victory. A slightly different version claims that the young runner chose to run through boggy land that slowed down the horse. The result was the same. Even worse, his sweetheart had watched the tragedy unfold and drowned herself in her misery. Her ghost remains, following the drum-beat of horse's hooves.

Buckland Brewer beside Bideford in Devon was the site for multiple hangings, and the ghosts remain here.

There are other stories, such as that of Azariah Pinney of Broadwindsor who stood in Monmouth's ranks. We have met him already, remember? Jeffreys ordered him deported to the West Indies until he learned that the family was well-connected as lace makers and landowners. Wealth and position counted as much then as it does now so rather than leave in chains and degradation, Pinney sailed as a free man. He furthered his family business in the Caribbean and lived like a colonial king. Those without means were not so fortunate as the rich. In Corscombe in Dorset a baker's dozen of men was executed, their corpses dipped in pitch and displayed as a warning to others.

The authorities rewarded those who helped them. A man named George Penne of Weston Manor was granted a hundred of the captives as remuneration for supporting the King. Penne promptly sold them his new property into slavery in the Americas; others did likewise.

Judge Jeffreys has left a host of memories and legends. There is the story of the seventy-year-old Lady Alice Lisle from Ellingham in Hampshire who was found guilty of helping two men suspected of supporting Monmouth. Legend says that Jeffries sentenced her to be burned to death, which indicates the reputation he had. In the event, she was beheaded instead and now roams around as a headless ghost.

The town of Frome has dark memories of the Rising as well, for Monmouth is reputed to have stayed in Cork Street, and many victims were said to have been hanged, drawn and quartered at Gore Hedge, near Bath Street. Sometimes, if the wind is down and traffic noises do not intervene, the horrible sound of men choking to death can still be heard in the area. One hundred and forty executions are claimed to have contaminated the Great Hall of Taunton Castle after the Bloody Assizes. That total seems exaggerated, but even so, this place has a grim atmosphere. A building has stood on the site for around a thousand years, and Jeffreys' ghost is only one of the spirits that add interest to the place. A Grey Lady, a Cavalier and a mysterious woman keep the merciless judge company.

Jeffries' ghost remains in Lyme Regis, where the authorities executed a dozen men. Jeffreys spent time on Broad Street in a long-demolished house. The story claims that he is seen chewing on a bone dripping with blood. He has a busy and much-travelled spirit which can also be seen or felt at his house in Walton on Thames as well as in the middle of Dorchester and Lydford in Devon, occasionally accompanied by the death agonies of some of the men he condemned and sometimes in the form of a black pig. Jeffreys must be the man with the most ghosts in England as patrons of the White Hart Hotel in Exeter have also seen him.

When Orange William and Mary Stuart landed in England to start the so-called Glorious Revolution, Jeffreys tried to flee the country. Somebody identified him as he hid in a Wapping pub, and a mob gathered to lynch him, as he had hanged so many in his career. Jeffreys escaped, to shelter in the Tower of London, a suitably grim spot for him. He died there in April 1689 of kidney disease.

People will forever associate the cruelty of Judge Jeffreys with Monmouth's Rebellion and the Battle of Sedgemoor, but the battlefield itself remains the haunt of those who dared their lives. Ghostly voices float across the moor, especially on misty days, trying to persuade the opposition to surrender or change sides. Monmouth's men, long dead, can still be heard along the banks of the River Carey challenging the royal troops to 'come over and fight.' The royal troops did so in their own time, but not before they had shattered the rebels with cannon fire to which there could be no reply. Monmouth's men had no artillery. There is the shimmering shape of long-gone cavalry and Monmouth himself, hunched and broken by defeat as he escapes the massacre of his soldiers. There are also the screams of the dying and the neighing of horses, the shape of hiding fugitives and overall an atmosphere of despair and frustration.

Monmouth was captured a few days after the battle, sleeping in a ditch. While so many of his followers were dying, he tried to plead for clemency but was taken to Tower Hill and beheaded. As he stood beside the block, he handed six guineas to his executioner with the words:

'Here are six guineas for you and do not hack me as you did my Lord Russell. I have heard you struck him four or five times. If you strike me twice, I cannot promise you not to stir.'

It was said that Jack Ketch botched the job.

Macauley gives graphic details of the execution where the first blow of the axe succeeded only in inflicting a minor wound and Monmouth rose up to 'look reproachfully at the executioner.' Ketch tried again and again without success as Monmouth suffered on the block. With the crowd yelling in anger, Ketch dropped his axe. 'I cannot do it,' he said, 'my heart fails me.'

As the crowd bayed for Ketch's blood, he tried again, failed and finished the job with a knife. He had to be escorted away from the crowd for his own protection as Monmouth lay, finally decapitated in a spreading pool of royal blood.

But that blood was too precious to waste as some of the crowd surged forward to soak handkerchiefs and sundry pieces of cloth in it. Monmouth, the leader of a failed revolt, was now a Protestant martyr. Then the stories began. The man who Ketch had just butchered to death was not Monmouth but an imposter, a sort of whipping-boy while Monmouth was safe in France, a king over-the-water waiting to return in glory. Another version claims that King James VII and II was not keen on executing his nephew so ordered him to be imprisoned in France instead. King Louis XIV, another relative, had a mask placed on his face so he could not be recognised - and the legend of the Man in the Iron Mask was born.

There is yet another story that is so incredible that it may be true. Some said that there was no portrait of Monmouth so after all the trouble taken to hack off his head, it was recovered and sewed back on so that a painter could create a proper royal portrait of the now deceased traitor.

The legacy of Monmouth's Rising continued, slowly fading, for centuries. There was a story that even Queen Victoria was affected. After the mass executions, the town of Bridgewater became so opposed to royalty than when Good Queen Vic's train steamed through she had to haul down the blinds. Her Majesty was not amused by Bridgewater and the town disapproved of royalty.

Jeffreys may be consoled by the fact that he is not the only hanging judge to have a ghost roaming the country. The ghost of Judge Page is apparently stuffed into a beer barrel every midsummer night at the village of Steeple

Aston. Not only that but a hundred owls then chase him around the pond. The owls are said to be the ghosts of widows of men he hanged. Page was an unpopular and unpleasant man whose memorial is in the local churchyard. If you look closely you will see that his wife is not wearing a wedding ring; the story goes that the judge did not pay the stonemason the agreed amount so in revenge he did not complete the sculpture; the judge is therefore living – or dying – in sin for eternity.

Chapter Twenty
Crop Circles and Farewell

One last piece of strangeness and this book will end;
o One final farewell that encompassed England and
stretches to the uttermost limits of the galaxy, or perhaps
the nearest public house. England is the original home of
crop circles, that array of strange shapes that appeared in
fields, baffled locals and scientists and thrilled Ufologists
and others who hoped for proof of life in other planets.
Are they hoaxes or are they the marks left by interplan-
etary visitors who were either too shy to say 'hi' or took
one look at the mess the world is making of this world
and decided to leave quickly?

For those who have not come across the term before, a
crop circle is a strange pattern created in a field, usually
of some grain such as wheat, by flattening the crop. No
doubt the local farmers have their own word or words
for these phenomena and the people who make them,
from whatever world they come. It was a man named
Colin Andrews who coined the phrase 'crop circles' in
the 1980s when a host of such occurrences struck Eng-

land. Most seem to occur in the south of the country and are often relatively near ancient sites such as Stonehenge. That could mean there is a cultural connection, or the makers of these rings wish them to be easily found by some of the many visitors to such places.

One major thing has always puzzled those who believe that aliens caused the circles. Why don't they drop directly outside the Houses of Parliament and make themselves known? If they have travelled millions of miles across the galaxy to visit planet Earth, why waste time wandering around a field in Wiltshire or abducting some poor man who works in the local Asdas? Why not go right to the heart of the place and talk to the boss? Unless the circles themselves are messages, writing from beyond the stars with a language that we do not as yet understand. That is unlikely, given the technology required even to reach another planet.

So are they all hoaxes? Probably, and only when and if scientific evidence comes to light to prove they are not hoaxes will opinions alter. It is possible that a small number of highly skilled people, working with cord and boards, have been responsible for a large number of these circles. The circles appear overnight when most sensible people are in bed or working night shift in essential jobs, and there is no doubt that human hands made the original circles in the late 1970s. The creators, Dave Chorley and Douglas Bower, admitted as much.

However, nature can play strange tricks with humanity, and dust devils, whirlwinds and the like can easily create un-natural seeming patterns in fields. Perhaps blaming tricksters for every crop circle is unfair. Mother Nature in one form or other may have leaned out her not-always gentle fingers to ease down the odd few thousand stalks of wheat. Of course, there is a vague possibility that creatures from the planet Zog have stopped to re-fuel or look at the scenery or have a quiet pint in the local pub, and if one such spacecraft should make itself known, all the speculation and theories will have to be re-written. There is also the possibility that fairies made the circles...

And with those thoughts on strange crop circles, this book will close. It has been a look at only some of the strange things that make up the fabric of England, from highwaymen to pub names, sports to haunted places, dancing stones to some unpleasant people. It only touched the surface. There is much more strangeness in England. The best way to find out is to leave the car and walk, talk to the locals and ask. People like to show off their local curiosities. Strange, that.

Jack Strange

Printed in Great Britain
by Amazon